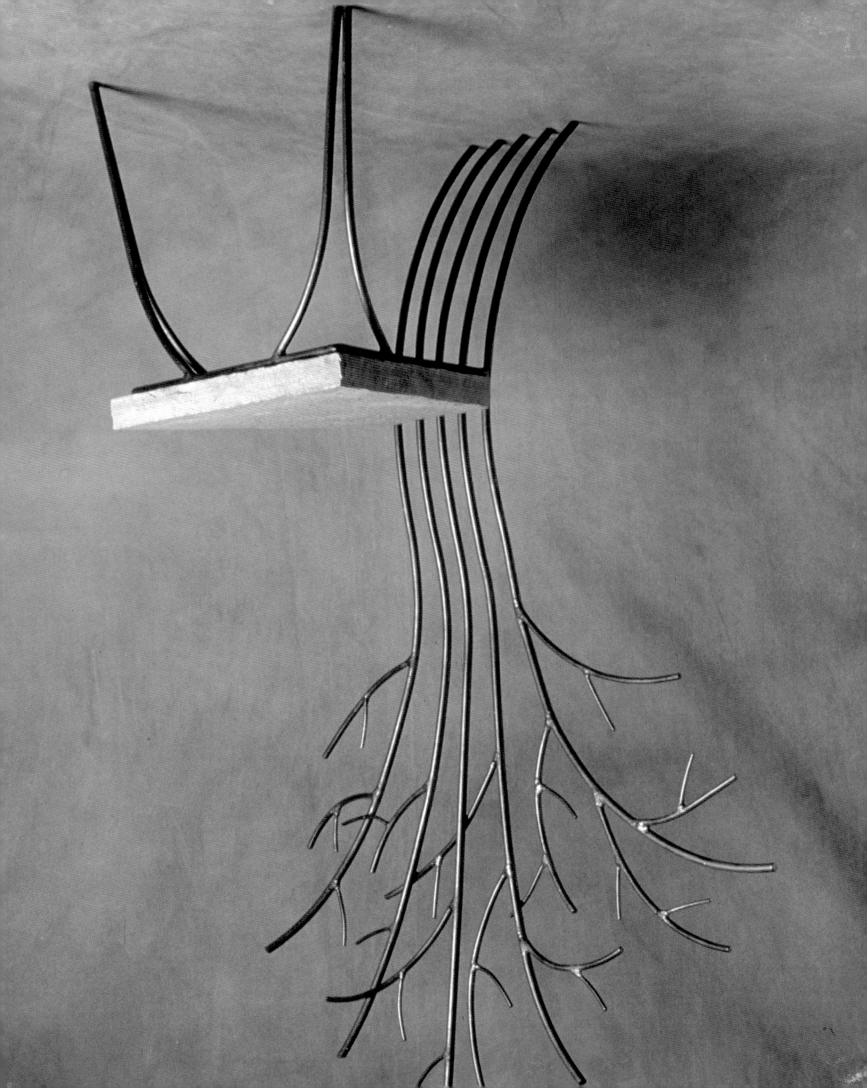

GRAPHIS PRODUCT DESIGN 2

. . . .

AN INTERNATIONAL SELECTION OF THE BEST IN PRODUCT DESIGN

EIN INTERNATIONALER ÜBERBLICK ÜBER DAS BESTE PRODUKTDESIGN

UN PANORAMA INTERNATIONAL DU DESIGN DE PRODUITS

EDITED BY • HERAUSGEGEBEN VON • EDITÉ PAR:

B. MARTIN PEDERSEN

PUBLISHER AND CREATIVE DIRECTOR: B. MARTIN PEDERSEN

EDITORS: MEL BYARS, CLARE HAYDEN, HEINKE JENSSEN

ASSOCIATE EDITORS: DANIEL IMAL, PEGGY CHAPMAN

PRODUCTION DIRECTOR: JOHN JEHEBER

GRAPHIS INC.

COVER • PRODUCT DESIGN BY ARCHITECTURE + DESIGN

OPPOSITE • DESIGN BY LELA EMMONS, STUDIO OZ

CONTENTS

INHALT

SOMMAIRE

REMARKS

ANMERKUNGEN

ANNOTATIONS

WE EXTEND OUR HEARTFELT THANKS TO CONTRIBUTORS THROUGHOUT THE WORLD WHO HAVE MADE IT POSSIBLE TO PUBLISH A WIDE AND INTERNATIONAL SPECTRUM OF THE BEST WORK IN THIS FIELD.

ENTRY INSTRUCTIONS FOR ALL GRAPHIS BOOKS MAY BE REQUESTED FROM:
GRAPHIS INC.
141 LEXINGTON AVENUE
NEW YORK, NY 10016-8193

UNSER DANK GILT DEN EINSENDERN AUS ALLER WELT, DIE ES UNS DURCH IHRE BEITRÄGE ERMÖGLICHT HABEN, EIN BREITES, INTERNATIONALES SPEKTRUM DER BESTEN ARBEITEN ZU VERÖFFENTLICHEN.

TEILNAHMEBEDINGUNGEN FÜR DIE GRAPHIS-BÜCHER SIND ERHÄLTLICH BEIM:
GRAPHIS INC.
141 LEXINGTON AVENUE
NEW YORK, NY 10016-8193

TOUTE NOTRE RECONNAISSANCE VA AUX DESIGNERS DU MONDE ENTIER DONT LES ENVOIS NOUS ONT PERMIS DE CONSTITUER UN VASTE PANORAMA INTERNATIONAL DES MEILLEURES CRÉATIONS.

LES MODALITÉS D'INSCRIPTION PEUVENT ÊTRE OBTENUES AUPRÈS DE:
GRAPHIS INC.
141 LEXINGTON AVENUE
NEW YORK, NY 10016-8193

OPPOSITE • DESIGN BY JOE GUZMÁN

FOLLOWING PAGE • DESIGN BY IDEO PRODUCT DEVELOPMENT FOR GALAXY BRANDS

PAGE 240 • DESIGN BY MAC FARRIOR. PHOTO BY MICHAEL TRAISTER

INTRODUCTION

EINLEITUNG

INTRODUCTION

Things, Objects, and Icons

"Things, objects, and icons" is Paola Antonelli's succinct hierarchical organization of the stuff in our lives. As the associate curator in the exalted Architecture and Design Department of The Museum of Modern Art in New York, there are few more aware of the artificial stratification system most of us use to classify our possessions than she. She will tell you that the world of things is a democratic universe. ■ Unfortunately, the democracy of things is undermined by the very people who use them. We all categorize and evaluate the stuff of our material culture, maybe even when we find the reverence for things abhorrent. Employing Ms. Antonelli's taxonomy, we take for granted utilitarian "things," such as wooden Faber Castell pencils. We respect special "objects," such as plastic Parker pens. And we revere the "icons" we hold so dear, such as gold Mont Blanc pens. But let's not fool ourselves into believing that the cost of things, reflected by these examples, automatically creates their place in the hierarchy of stuff; money may be a far less significant factor in forming our judgment than we think. ■ The jarring inequities in the ranking of objects are to be seen everywhere every

MEL BYARS STUDIED JOURNALISM IN HIS NATIVE SOUTH CAROLINA BEFORE SERVING IN NEW YORK AS ART AND CREATIVE DIRECTOR FOR NUMEROUS PUBLISHERS AND ADVERTISING AGENCIES. HE WROTE *THE DESIGN ENCYCLOPEDIA* (1994) AND A SERIES OF BOOKS ON CONTEMPORARY APPLIED ART INCLUDING *50 CHAIRS: INNOVATIONS IN DESIGN AND MATERIALS* (1997). HE IS A CONTRIBUTOR TO *I.D.* AND *BLUEPRINT* MAGAZINES AND THE ARCHIVIST OF THE THÉRÈSE BONNEY PHOTOGRAPHY COLLECTION AT THE COOPER-HEWITT NATIONAL DESIGN MUSEUM. HE HAS BEEN A MAJOR CONTRIBUTOR OF 20TH-CENTURY OBJECTS TO THE MUSEUM'S PERMANENT COLLECTION.

day. For example, look at the two vases in this survey (pages 138 and 139). The one in fine white porcelain with a faux wood-carved surface was designed by a French person who studied economics, not design, at a French university for a venerable 150-year-old French firm. The other vase was produced in a new substance, aluminum, that even at 185 years old is an infant in the family of materials. This vase was made for an international firm according to minutely detailed, written and drawn instructions and was designed by someone who studied design. ∎ Yet the conundrum persists. The evaluation of objects is based as much on their specialness, or lack of it, as on aesthetics. And this is why, for example, neither of these vastly dissimilar vases is better than the other; they are merely different, albeit very different, not better. Both vessels hold flowers; both are individually special; and both possess high aesthetic values because arguably no more conceptual care was given to one than to the other. Design-thinking time and production time are not relevant to the value of conceptual caring or aesthetic value. ∎ These vases are only two of the many carefully chosen objects in Graphis Product Design 2 that represent work produced during the last three years by designers and manufacturers worldwide. The range is wide, from telephones to teapots, light fixtures to forks, attaché cases to automobiles. And none is better than the other. For example, since the two mirrors included in this survey (pages 120 and 121) have immensely dissimilar values, to grade one against the other would be to perform a silly and hopeless exercise. Their only common ground is their function: they are mirrors. ∎ The history that surrounds one of the mirrors (produced by the euonymus group, Inflate) reveals the most consequential trend in the design industry that has happened in any one country for decades. The country is Great Britain, and what has happened is that its designers, long thwarted by a conservative or non-existent manufacturing community or by an inferiority complex fed by poverty and an ignorant government, have begun to manufacture their own design work themselves. They no longer, like Tom Dixon, Ron Arad, Jasper Morrison, and others, have to go to Italy or elsewhere to have product ideas realized. Today, we see this British entrepreneurship being expressed across a wide spectrum of the applied arts (pages 76, 120, 171). And in Holland, where a handful of willing manufacturers have existed for a long time, a new breed of designers banded together in 1993 to form the manufacturing-promotion agency Droog, which means "dry" or, maybe in its best sense, "plain." Lamentably, the managers of the group are not paragons of organizational competence, but,

indeed, this may be said of many elsewhere. ∎ Some of the products here, such as the chair (page 73) made by a Droog-group member in macramé-woven and epoxy-soaked aramid and carbon-fiber rope, illustrate highly advanced technological experimentation. Others, like the inflatable objects (pages 62, 120 and 171), speak more of folly than science, even though they have cleverly manipulated plastic film. There is electronic equipment that informs us of the designers' ongoing quest for ergonomic solutions which marry sensuous forms with practical function. Notice the nonconservative use of color (page 29), considered taboo in yesterday's office but desirable in today's workplace. ∎ In lighting, where almost anything is possible, there are surprises: innovation, such as that found in the hanging lamp that incorporates ceramic foam (page 176), and the playful interpretation of traditional forms, like that revealed by the yellow see-through table lamp (page 172)—not your mother's living-room fixture. ∎ And, inevitably, green concerns proliferate, whether motivated by benevolence or, despicably, by fashion. No matter how well-meaning, the products of a haute-aesthetic mien that incorporate recycled materials or that center on other conservational concerns will appreciably do nothing to nurse a sick planet back to health. Their importance lies more in the quantum gesture they make, like the AIDS lapel ribbon, reminding us of significant conservational methods and other Earth-respecting methodologies found in more mundane product designs. For example, painless concessions might include the replacement of old toilets with those that flush smaller amounts of water, the use of hand-operated appliances like can openers and juicers (p146), and the purchase of Chambord-type coffee makers, jettisoning the ones that stay hot for hours and suck up electricity. ∎ Design solutions that include concerns about function, safety, thrift, and preservation can be so aligned as to be imperceptible. We no longer have to make serious sacrifices. And no longer must special provisions and money necessarily be factors all the time in the production of people-embracing objects. A dullard is ill-informed of the attributes and benefits a good object and asks only if it looks nice, if even that. Alas, most of us may still use aesthetic values and price as the major criteria for judging products while frequently being overwhelmed by the pressure to make the right choices. But hopefully the collection of products in this modest survey will serve to shift our focus from the pretty, the pleasing, the petty, and the predictable—all of which you can find here—to other qualities, like the innovative, the clever, the unique, and the salubrious—all here too.

- -
MEL BYARS GEGENSTÄNDE, OBJEKTE UND IKONEN
- -

«Gegenstände, Objekte und Ikonen» – diese Begriffe bezeichnen gemäss Paola Antonelli die Hierarchie der Dinge in unserem Leben. Sie ist Vize-Kuratorin der Abteilung für Architektur und Design des Museum of Modern Art in New York, und wer wüsste besser Bescheid über das System, das die meisten von uns anwenden, um unsere Besitztümer einzuordnen. Sie wird Ihnen sagen, dass die Welt der Dinge ein demokratisches Universum ist. ∎ Leider wird die Demokratie der Dinge von genau den Leuten, die sie verwenden, untergraben. Wir alle kategorisieren und bewerten die Dinge unserer materiellen Kultur, selbst

wenn wir die Verehrung von Dingen verabscheuen sollten. Wenden wir einmal Paola Antonellis Klassifikation an, dann betrachten wir Gebrauchsgegenstände wie Faber-Castell-Bleistifte aus Holz als selbstverständlich; respektieren spezielle Objekte wie Parker-Schreibgeräte aus Plastik und verehren die Ikonen, uns lieb gewordene Dinge wie die goldenen Mont-Blanc-Füllfederhalter. Wir sollten jedoch nicht meinen, dass die Kosten der Dinge, die bei den genannten Beispielen offensichtlich sind, automatisch ihren Platz in der Hierarchie der Dinge bestimmen; Geld könnte eine viel unbedeutendere Rolle bei unserer

MEL BYARS HAT IN SEINEM HEIMATSTAAT SOUTH CAROLINA JOURNALISMUS STUDIERT. DANACH HAT ER IN NEW YORK ALS ART DIRECTOR BZW. CREATIVE DIRECTOR FÜR VERSCHIEDENE VERLAGE UND WERBEAGENTUREN. GEARBEITET,. NACHDEM ER AN DER NEW SCHOOL FOR SOCIAL RESEARCH ANTHROPOLOGIE STUDIERT HATTE, BEFASSTE ER SICH MIT DESIGN-GESCHICHTE UND VERFASSTE *THE DESIGN ENCYCLOPEDIA* (1994) SOWIE EINE REIHE WEITERER BÜCHER U.A. *50 CHAIRS: INNOVATIONS IN DESIGN AND MATERIALS* (1997); WEITERE BÄNDE ÜBER TISCHE, LEUCHTEN UND PRODUKTE SIND IM DRUCK. MEL BYARS IST MITARBEITER DER ZEITSCHRIFTEN *I.D.* UND *BLUEPRINT*.

Beurteilung spielen, als wir gemeinhin annehmen. ■ Die eklatanten Ungleichheiten bei der Einordnung der Dinge manifestieren sich überall und jederzeit. Man schaue sich zum Beispiel die beiden Vasen auf S. 38 und 39 dieses Bandes an. Die eine, aus feinem weissen Porzellan mit einer holzschnittartigen Oberfläche, wurde für eine ehrwürdige, 150 Jahre alte französische Firma von einem Franzosen entworfen, der an einer französischen Universität Betriebswirtschaft studiert hat und nicht etwa Design. Die Vase wurde von französischen Kunsthandwerkern nach alten, traditionellen französischen Handwerksmethoden hergestellt. Es ist eine Vase, die mit der Stimme der Vergangenheit spricht. Wenn eine solche Vase auch einen noch so kleinen Fehler aufweist, wird sie zerstört und gelangt niemals in die Hände des Käufers. Die andere Vase ist aus einem neuen Material, Aluminium, das mit seiner 185jährigen Tadition unter den Materialien noch immer ein Neuling ist. Diese Vase wurde für eine internationale Firma nach in Wort und Bild genau festgelegten Vorschriften hergestellt. Entworfen wurde sie von jemandem, der Design studiert hat und in dem Land geboren wurde, in dem die Firma ihren Hauptsitz hat. Sie spricht die Sprache unserer Gegenwart, in der die meisten Dinge, genau wie diese Vase, von jemandem an einem Ort entworfen werden und dann an einem weit entfernten Ort von Fremden hergestellt werden, weil sie schnell und billig arbeiten. Die Vasen, die sie herstellen, haben unter Umständen Fehler, aber wenn diese Defekte nicht augenfällig sind, werden die meisten nicht zerstört sondern verkauft, weil kleinere Defekte in diesem Fall keine Rolle spielen. ■ Und doch bleibt es ein Rätsel. Die Bewertung von Dingen basiert ebenso auf ihrer Besonderheit – oder dem Fehlen einer solchen – wie auf der Ästhetik. Und das ist der Grund, warum zum Beispiel keine dieser sehr verschiedenen Vasen besser als die andere ist; sie sind nur verschieden, sehr verschieden, aber nicht besser oder schlechter. In beide Gefässe kann man Blumen hineinstellen, beide sind aussergewöhnlich, und beide haben ein hohes ästhetisches Niveau, weil beim Entwurf die gleiche Sorgfalt angewandt wurde. Die Zeit, die das Design und die Produktion in Anspruch nahmen, hat keinen Einfluss die Bewertung des Entwurfs und der Ästhetik. ■ Diese Vasen sind nur zwei Beispiele der vielen sorgfältig ausgewählten Objekte, die in Graphis Products by Design 2 vorgestellt werden, Arbeiten aus den letzten drei Jahren von Designern und Herstellern aus aller Welt. Das Spektrum ist breit, es reicht von Telephonen bis zu Teekannen, von Leuchten bis zu Gabeln, von Attaché-Koffern bis zu Autos. Und kein Objekt ist besser als das andere. Die beiden Spiegel zum Beispiel (S. 120 und 121) sind so extrem verschieden, dass der Versucch, einen Vergleich anzustellen, ein völlig sinnloses und hoffnungsloses Unterfangen wäre. Ihr einziger gemeinsamer Nenner ist ihre Funktion: es sind Spiegel. ■ Der eine Spiegel (hergestellt von der Gruppe Inflate) ist beispielhaft für ein konsequentes Vorgehen, das seit Jahrzehnten in keinem anderen Land in dieser Form beobachtet werden konnte. Der Ort des Geschehens ist Grossbritannien, wo Designer lange Zeit wegen der konservativen oder nicht vorhandenen Industrie Schwierigkeiten hatten, ihre Entwürfe zu realisieren. Sie haben reagiert und begonnen, die Herstellung selbst in die Hand zu nehmen, um nicht mehr wie seinerzeit Tom Dixon, Ron Arad, Jasper Morrison und andere nach Italien oder sonstwo hingehen zu müssen, damit ihre Produktideen ausgeführt werden. Heute manifestiert sich dieses britische Unternehmertum in einem breiten Spektrum der angewandten Künste (S. 76, 120 und 171). In Holland, wo es schon lange eine Handvoll sehr aufgeschlossener Hersteller gibt, hat sich 1993 eine neue Generation von Designern zusammengeschlossen, um die Herstellungsagentur Droog zu gründen. «Droog» bedeutet eigentlich «trocken», was in diesem Fall vielleicht besser mit «schlicht» umschrieben wird. Leider sind die Manager der Gruppe nicht gerade Organisationstalente, aber das lässt sich auch von vielen anderen behaupten. ■ Einige der hier gezeigten Produkte, wie der Stuhl (S. 73) eines Mitglieds der Droog-Gruppe, sind Beispiele von Experimenten auf höchstem technischen Niveau. Andere, wie die aufblasbaren Objekte (S. 62, 120 und 171), haben eher mit ausgeflippten Einfällen als mit Technik zu tun, wenn auch der Plastikfilm eine kluge Lösung ist. Es gibt elektronische Geräte, die das Ergebnis gründlicher ergonomischer Studien sind und sinnliche Formen mit praktischem Nutzen vereinen. Man beachte den ungewöhnlichen Einsatz von Farben (S. 29), die in den Büros von gestern nicht vorstellbar, an den heutigen Arbeitsplätzen aber sehr willkommen sind. ■ Bei den Leuchten, bei denen so ziemlich alles möglich ist, gibt es Überraschungen: Innovationen wie bei der Hängelampe (S. 176), die eine spielerische Interpretation traditioneller Formen ist, wie auch bei der transparenten, gelben Tischlampe (S. 172), die nichts mit der Wohnzimmerlampe Ihrer Mutter zu tun hat. ■ Umweltaspekte, ob aus Überzeugung oder weil es Mode ist, spielen allenthalben eine Rolle. Wenn auch gut gemeint, werden Produkte, die wiederverwertete Materialien enthalten oder nach anderen umweltfreundlichen Gesichtspunkten hergestellt wurden, nicht viel dazu beitragen können, einen kranken Planeten zu heilen. Ihre Bedeutung liegt in der Geste, indem sie an Schonung der Ressourcen und andere bedeutende umweltfreundliche Methoden erinnern, die in der Herstellung und Konzeption einfacherer Produkt-Designs zum Ausdruck kommt. Zugeständnisse, die kaum wehtun, wären zum Beispiel neue WCs, deren Spülung weniger Wasser verbraucht, Küchengeräte, z.B. Dosenöffner, die man von Hand betätigt, oder Kaffeemaschinen, die nicht stundenlang heissgehalten werden und damit weniger Strom verbrauchen. ■ Überlegungen über Funktion, Sicherheit, Sparsamkeit und Umwelterhaltung müssen in den Produkten nicht unbedingt für das Auge sichtbar werden. Wir müssen keine grossen Zugeständnisse machen, und auch eine spezielle Beschaffenheit oder Geld müssen nicht unbedingt immer ausschlaggebende Faktoren bei der Herstellung konsumentenfreundlicher Gegenstände sein. Ein Dummkopf weiss nichts von den Eigenschaften und Vorteilen eines guten Objekts und fragt höchstens, ob es hübsch aussieht. Nun mögen für die meisten noch immer die Ästhetik und der Preis bei der Beurteilung von Produkten die Hauptkriterien sein, und zwar immer unter dem Druck, die richtigen Entscheidungen treffen zu wollen. Hoffentlich werden die in diesem Band gezeigten Produkte dazu beitragen, dass nicht nur das Hübsche, Gefällige, Belanglose und Voraussehbare beachtet wird – das alles lässt sich in diesem Band auch finden –, sondern andere Qualitäten wie das Innovative, das Clevere, das Einzigartige und das Gesunde, das hier ebenfalls gezeigt wird.

MEL BYARS EST NÉ EN CAROLINE DU SUD OÙ IL A ÉTUDIÉ LE JOURNALISME AVANT D'ENTAMER SA CARRIÈRE PROFESSIONNELLE À NEW YORK. IL A TRAVAILLÉ POUR DIVERS ÉDITEURS TELS QUE PRENTICE-HALL ET MACGRAW-HILL, AINSI QUE POUR DES AGENCES DE PUBLICITÉ, DONT LEBER KATZ PARTNERS. APRÈS DES ÉTUDES EN ANTHROPOLOGIE, IL SE TOURNE VERS L'HISTOIRE DU DESIGN. IL EST L'AUTEUR DE THE DESIGN ENCYCLOPEDIA (1994) ET D'UNE SÉRIE D'OUVRAGES SUR LES ARTS APPLIQUÉS CONTEMPORAINS, DONT 50 CHAIRS: INNOVATIONS IN DESIGN AND MATERIALS (1997). D'AUTRES LIVRES SUR LES TABLES, LES LUMINAIRES ET LES PRODUITS VONT PARAÎTRE PROCHAINEMENT.

«Choses, objets et icônes», telle est l'organisation hiérarchique succincte utilisée par Paola Antonelli pour classer tout ce qui nous entoure au quotidien. En tant que conservatrice adjointe du département d'architecture et de design du Musée d'Art moderne de New York, elle est tout à fait consciente du système de stratification artificiel appliqué par la plupart d'entre nous pour classer nos possessions. Elle vous dira que le monde des objets est un univers démocratique. ■ Malheureusement, la démocratie des choses est justement sapée par ceux qui les utilisent. Nous classons et évaluons tous les objets de notre culture matérielle, même si nous réprouvons le fait de vénérer un objet. Si nous nous en référons à la taxinomie de Paola Antonelli, les «choses» utilitaires, comme des crayons en bois Faber Castell, nous paraissent tout à fait naturelles. Nous respectons les «objets» spéciaux – des stylos Parker par exemple – et nous vénérons les «icônes», une plume Mont Blanc plaquée or, qui ont su gagner notre affection. Mais ne nous y trompons pas, ce n'est pas le prix des objets, à l'image de ces exemples, qui détermine automatiquement la place occupée dans cette hiérarchie; l'argent influence beaucoup moins notre jugement que nous ne voulons bien le croire. ■ Les inégalités criantes dans la classification des objets sont visibles partout, chaque jour. Regardez par exemple les deux vases présentés dans cet ouvrage en page 38 et 39. L'un, en fine porcelaine blanche, a été dessiné par un Français pour le compte d'une vénérable entreprise de 150 ans. Cet artiste a étudié les sciences économiques et non le design dans une université française. Fabriqué avec de l'aluminium, un des petits derniers dans la famille des matériaux même s'il existe depuis 185 ans, le deuxième vase a été créé pour une société internationale selon des instructions très précises, présentées sous forme de textes ou de dessins. Son concepteur a étudié le design.. ■ L'énigme n'est pourtant pas résolue. Pour évaluer des objets, nous nous basons sur leurs spécificités – s'ils en ont – et sur l'esthétique. Et, pour cette raison, aucun de ces deux vases, largement dissemblables, n'est meilleur que l'autre. Ils sont différents, c'est tout. Tous deux sont destinés à contenir des fleurs, tous deux sont spéciaux et possèdent une grande valeur esthétique parce que le même soin a été apporté à l'un et à l'autre lors de leur conception. Le temps nécessaire au design et à la production ne sont pas déterminants pour leur valeur conceptuelle ou esthétique. Ces vases ne représentent que deux exemples parmi les objets soigneusement sélectionnés pour Graphis Products by Design 2, des travaux produits au cours des trois dernières années par des designers et des fabricants du monde entier. La palette des objets présentés est large, des téléphones aux théières, des luminaires aux fourchettes, en passant par des porte-documents et des véhicules. Et aucun n'est meilleur que l'autre. Les deux miroirs illustrés dans cet ouvrage (p. 120 et 121), par exemple, sont tellement différents que les classer dans un catégorie serait un exercice stupide et sans espoir. Leur seul point commun, c'est leur fonction: ce sont des miroirs. ■ L'histoire entourant l'un de ces deux miroirs (produit par le groupe Inflate) témoigne d'une approche conséquente qui n'a pu être observée dans un aucun autre pays au cours des dernières décennies. Ce pays, c'est la Grande-Bretagne, et ses designers, dont les projets ont longtemps été contrecarrés par une communauté de fabricants conservateurs ou inexistants, ont commencé à fabriquer leurs propres créations pour ne plus devoir, comme Tom Dixon, Ron Arad ou Jasper

Morrison et tant d'autres, aller en Italie où ailleurs pour voir leurs idées se matérialiser. Aujourd'hui, cet esprit entrepreneurial britannique s'exprime à travers de nombreuses disciplines des arts appliqués (p. 76, 120 et 171). En Hollande, où un petit nombre de fabricants volontaires a longtemps existé, des designers ont décidé d'unir leurs efforts en 1993 et ont fondé l'agence de fabrication Droog, qui signifie «sec» ou «épuré» dans le meilleur sens du terme. Malheureusement, les directeurs du groupe ne sont pas des parangons en matière d'organisation, mais cette remarque pourrait s'appliquer à bien d'autres personnes. ■ Certains des produits présentés ici, comme cette chaise (p. 73) créée par un membre du groupe Droog, sont le fruit d'expérimentations technologiques avancées. D'autres, à l'image des objets gonflables (p. 62, 120 et 171), ont plus trait à la folie qu'à la technologie. Il y a bien sûr les équipements électroniques qui témoignent de la recherche constante des designers pour trouver des solutions ergonomiques mariant fonctionnalité et esthétique. Notez également l'utilisation inhabituelle de couleurs (page 92) qui aurait été impensable dans les bureaux d'hier, mais qui constitue un plus pour les postes de travail d'aujourd'hui. ■ Dans le domaine des luminaires, où presque tout est possible, il y a d'heureuses surprises: des innovations comme cette lampe (p. 176), une interprétation ludique des formes traditionnelles, ou encore cette lampe de table jaune et transparente (p. 172) – qui n'a sans doute rien à voir avec la lampe du salon de votre mère. ■ Et, phénomène inévitable, les considérations écologiques sont largement prises en considération que soit par conviction ou par mode. Et, même si l'intention est honorable, ces produits, qui contiennent des matériaux recyclables ou sont fabriqués selon des processus écologiques, ne changeront sans doute pas grand-chose aux maux de la planète. En eux, il faut voir un geste, un clin d'œil, dans la mesure où ils nous rappellent qu'il existe des moyens de préserver les ressources naturelles et des méthodes de fabrication écologiques qui trouvent d'ailleurs leur expression dans les produits design. Il serait facile de faire certaines concessions, comme de remplacer, par exemple, les anciennes toilettes par de nouvelles, beaucoup plus économes du point de vue de la consommation en eau, de créer des appareils ménagers que l'on utilise avec ses mains, je pense là à un ouvre-boîtes, ou encore des machines à café qui ne restent pas allumées durant des heures et consomment de l'électricité. ■ En matière de design, les réflexions faites sur la fonction, la sécurité, l'aspect économique et le respect de l'environnement ne doivent pas forcément être visibles à l'œil nu. Et les considérations financières ou une autre caractéristique ancrée dans les esprits ne doit pas non plus toujours être un facteur décisif pour la fabrication d'un produit. Un imbécile ignore les caractéristiques et les avantages d'un objet de qualité et se demande, tout au plus, si c'est beau. Certes, pour nombre de personnes l'esthétique et le prix continuent sans doute à constituer les principaux critères lors de l'évaluation d'un produit dans la mesure où elles se sentent obligées de faire le bon choix. Il reste à espérer que les produits présentés dans cet ouvrage contribueront à faire en sorte que l'on n'attache plus uniquement de l'importance à ce qui est beau, plaisant, mignon et prévisible – de tels exemples figurent naturellement aussi dans ce livre –, mais aussi à ce qui est novateur, intelligent, unique et sain – là aussi, nous vous en livrons quelques beaux spécimens.

PRODUCT

DESIGN

TWO

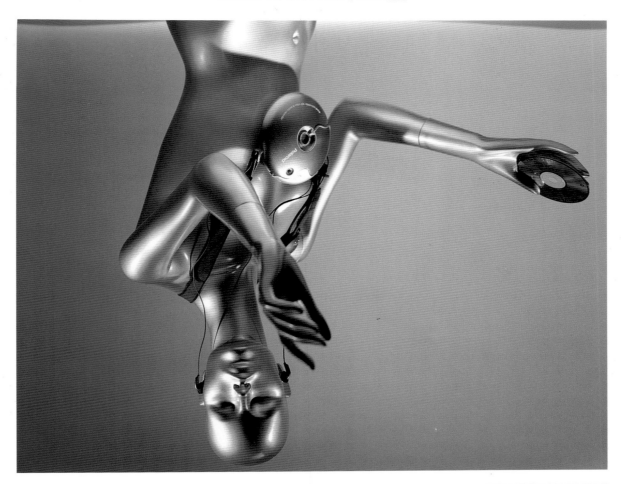

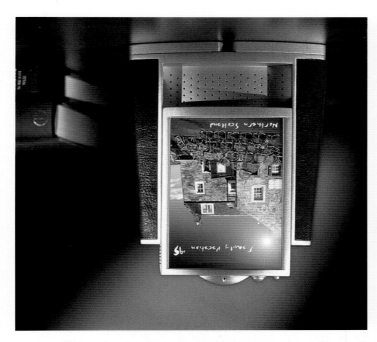

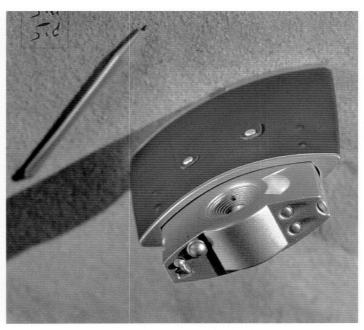

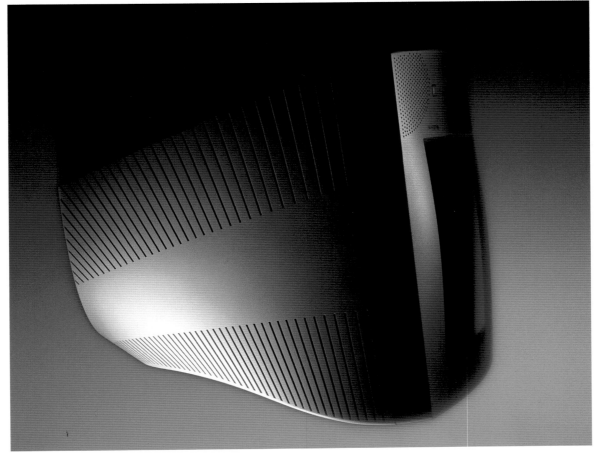

(Top) **VOID** *NEC Electronics* ■ (Bottom) **IDEO PRODUCT DEVELOPMENT** *Samsung Electronics*

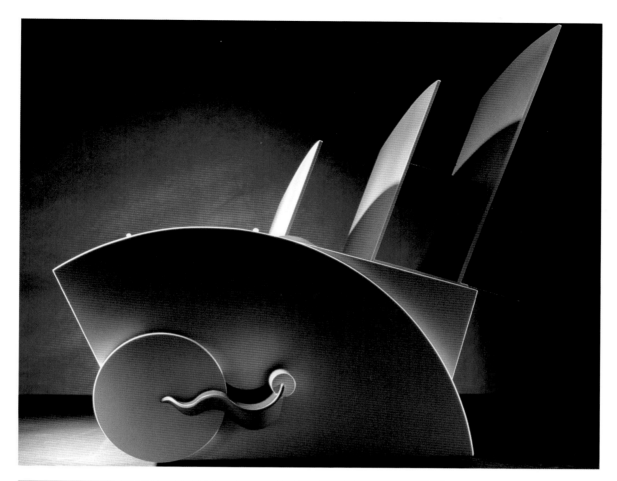

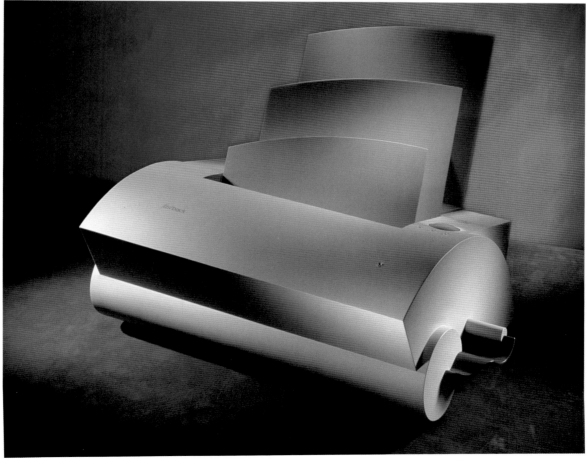

KASOM DESIGN *Powis Parker Company*

ELECTRONICS

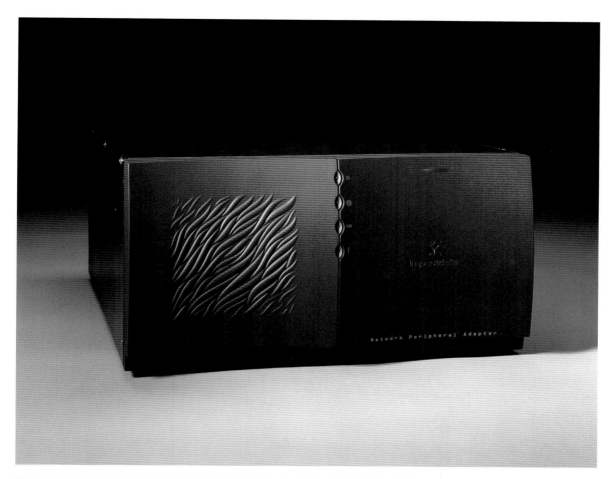

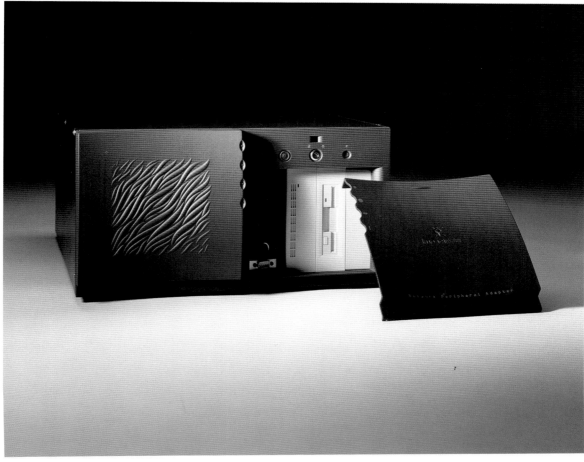

ASHCRAFT DESIGN *Impactdata*

PI DESIGN *Climax/ITC*

ELECTRONICS

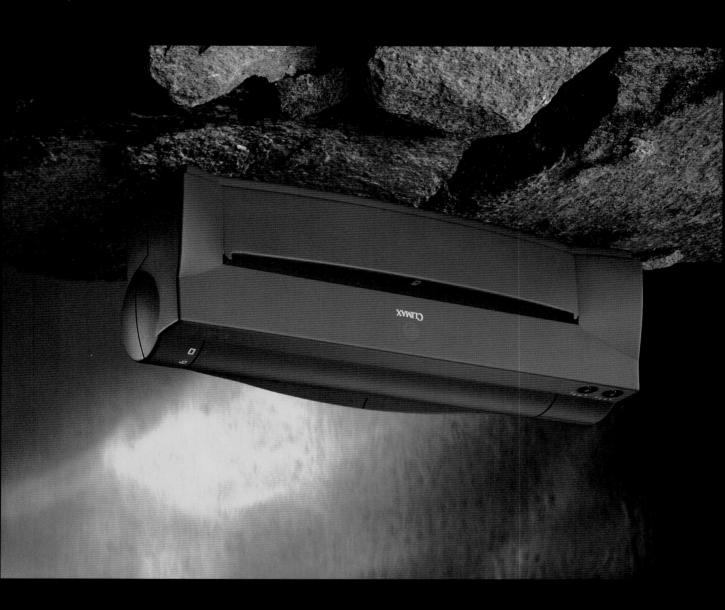

PI DESIGN *Climax/ITC*

2. 8

ELECTRONICS

HAUSER, INC. *Datametrics Corporation*

FROGDESIGN, INC. *Acer America Corporation*

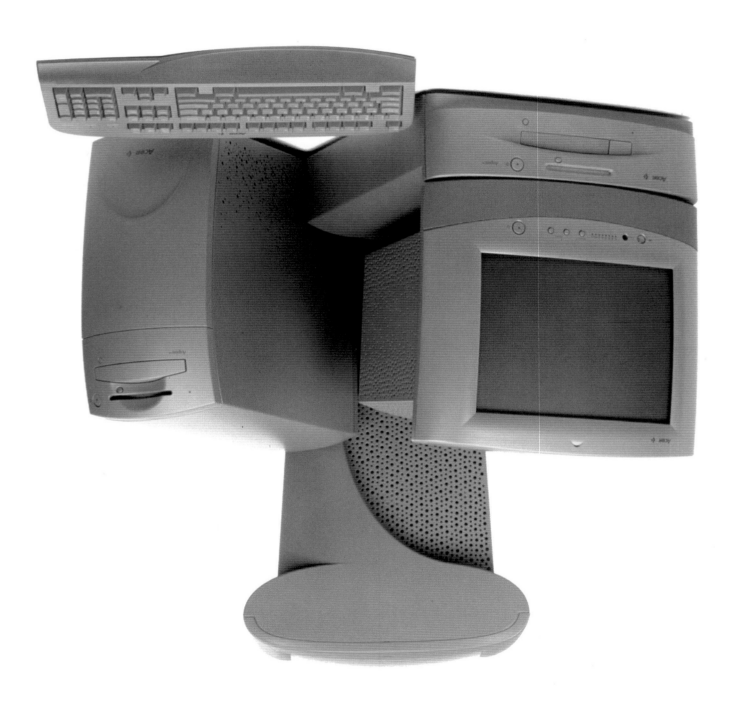

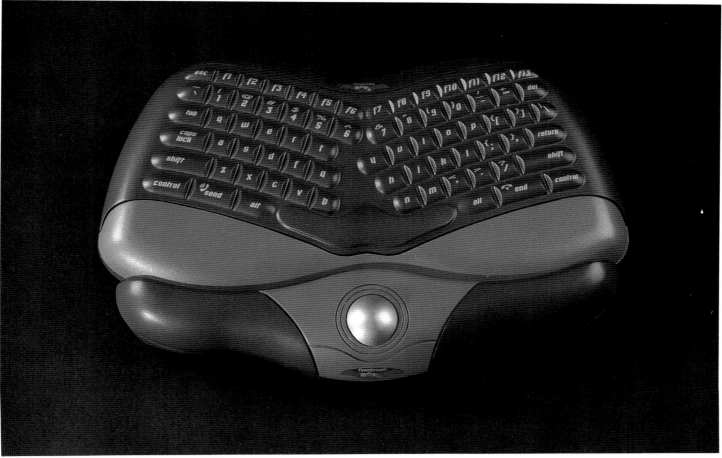

DESIGNDESIGN *Comstream*

ELECTRONICS

FROGDESIGN, INC. *Macworld*

FROGDESIGN, INC. *Astralink Technology PTE Ltd.*

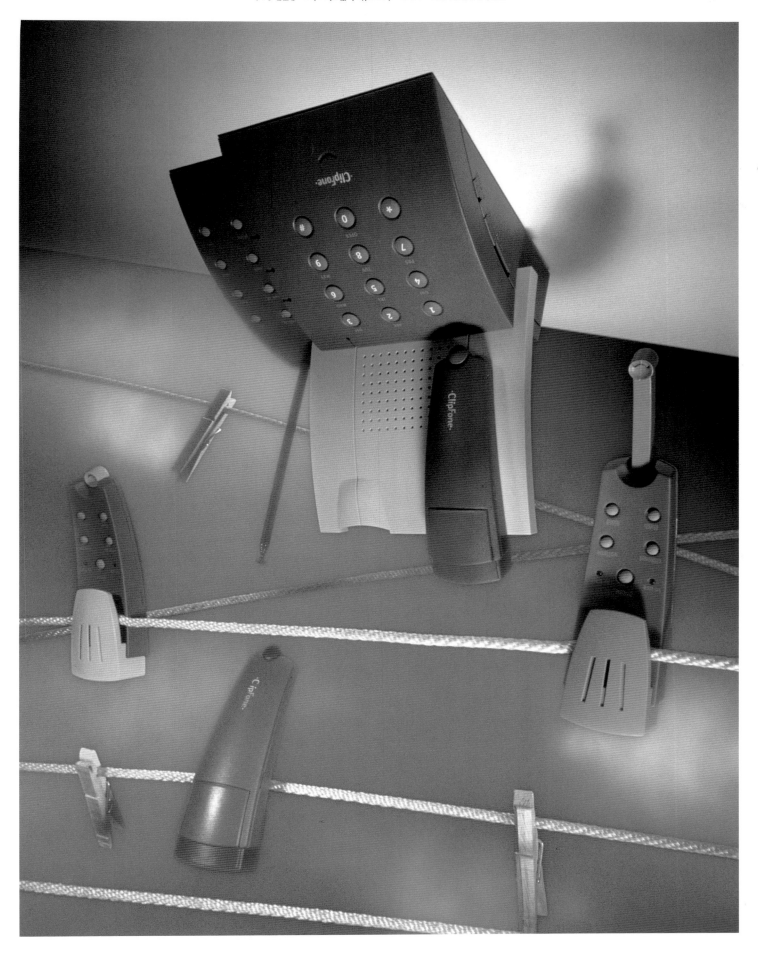

FROGDESIGN, INC. *Astralink Technology PTE Ltd.*

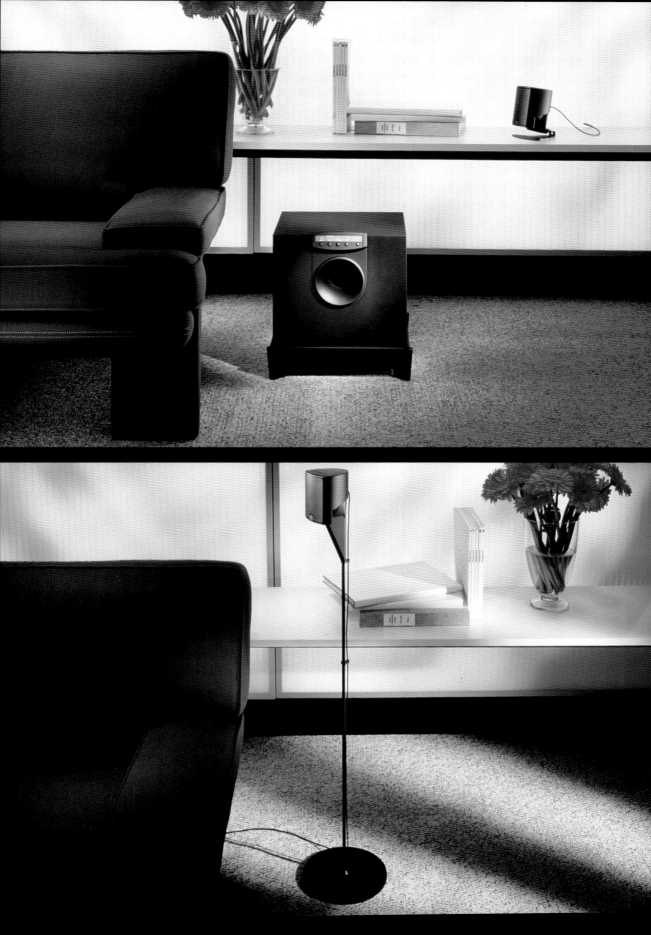

(This spread) **FITCH INC.** *JBL*

(This page) RKS DESIGN, INC. Harman Interactive Group/JBL. ■ (Opposite page) ASHCRAFT DESIGN Infinity

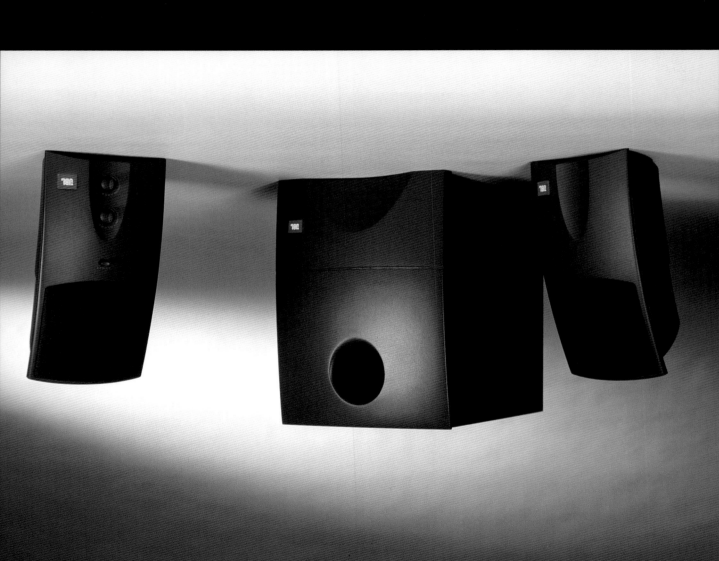

(This page) **FROGDESIGN, INC.** *Seagate Technology* ■ *(Opposite page)* **LUNAR DESIGN** *Silicon Graphics*

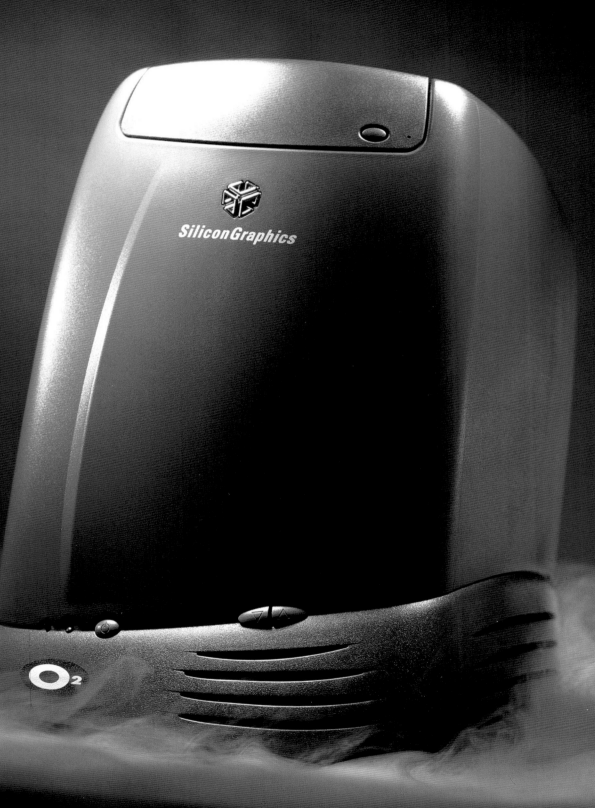

DESIGN EDGE Apple Computer Inc.

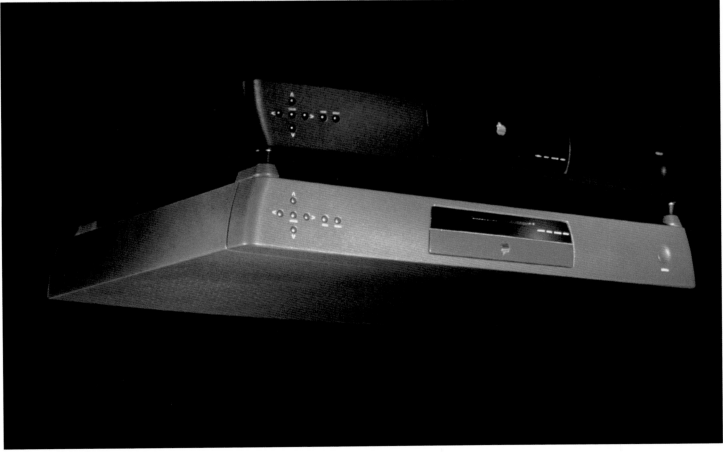

DESIGN EDGE Apple Computer Inc.

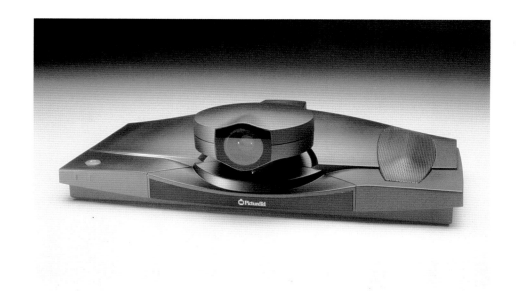

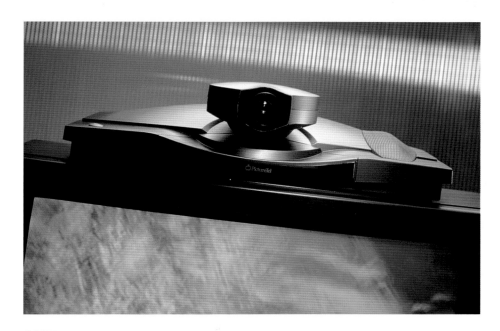

GVO INC. *PictureTel*

INTERFORM *Astounding Technologies*

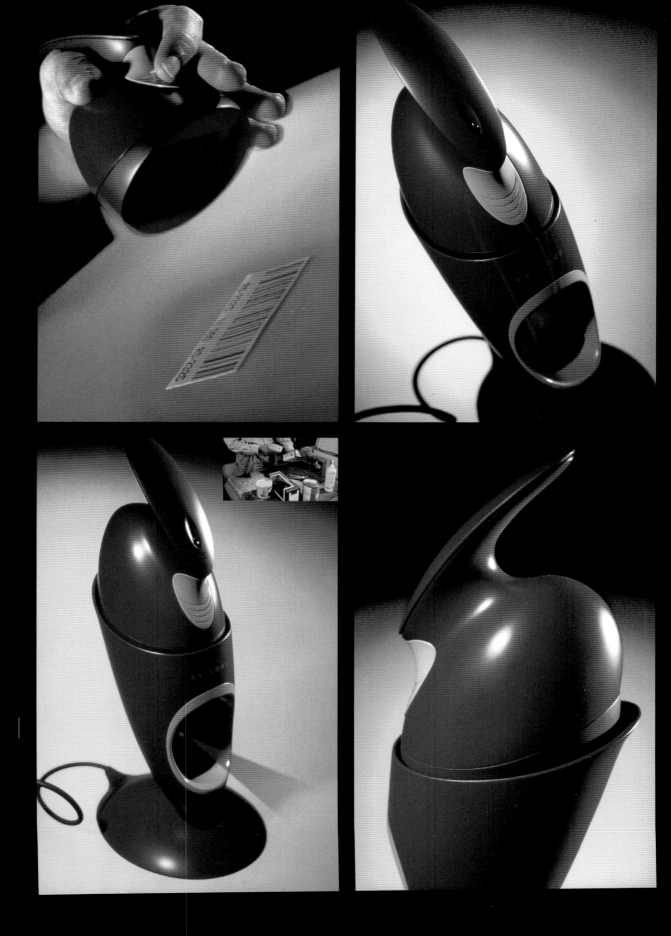

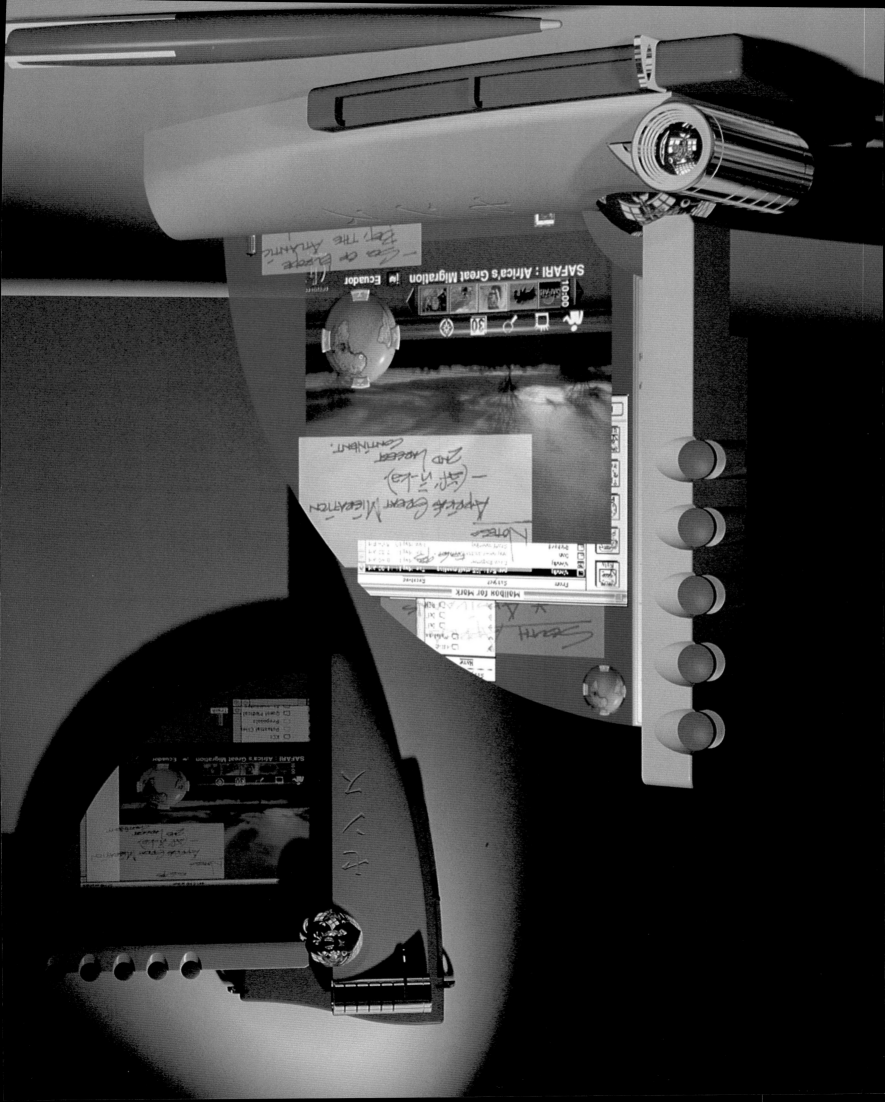

(Opposite page) **DESIGN EDGE** *IDEC* ■ *(This page)* **PHILIPS DESIGN (IN-HOUSE)**

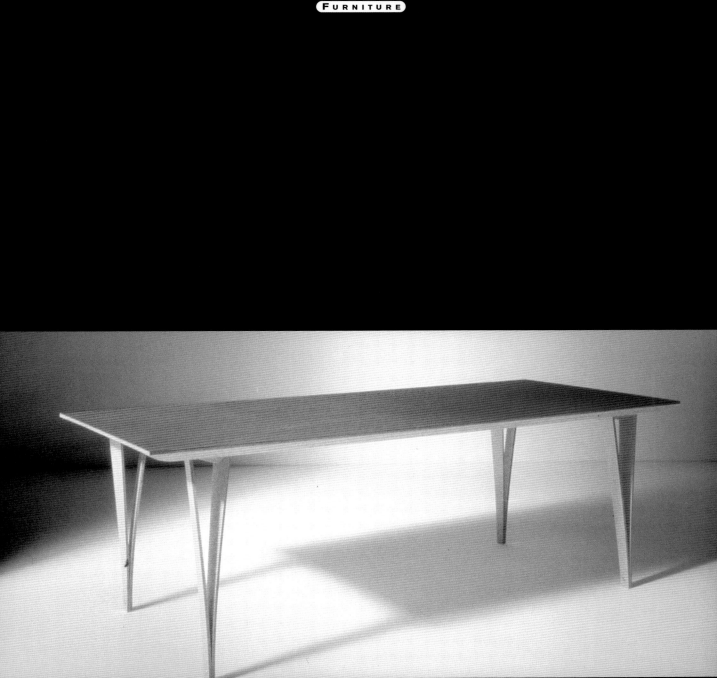

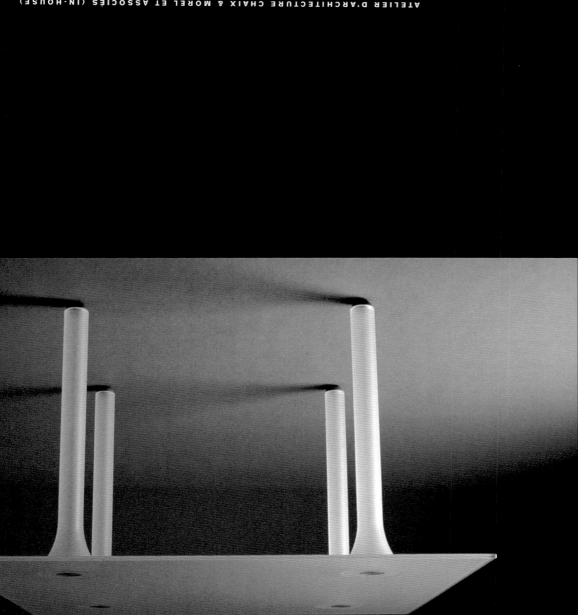

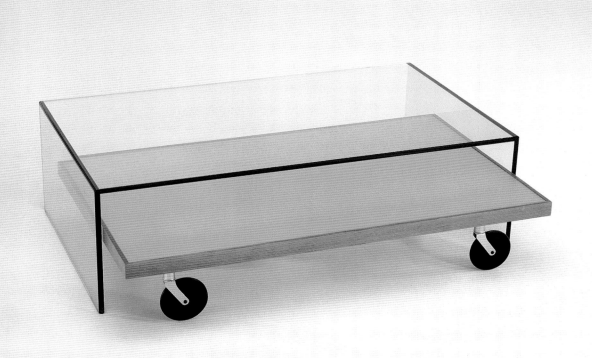

(This spread) **JEAN NOUVEL** *Unifor, S.p.A.*

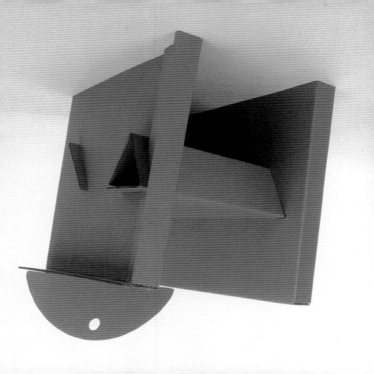

ATELIER BORIS BALLY (IN-HOUSE)

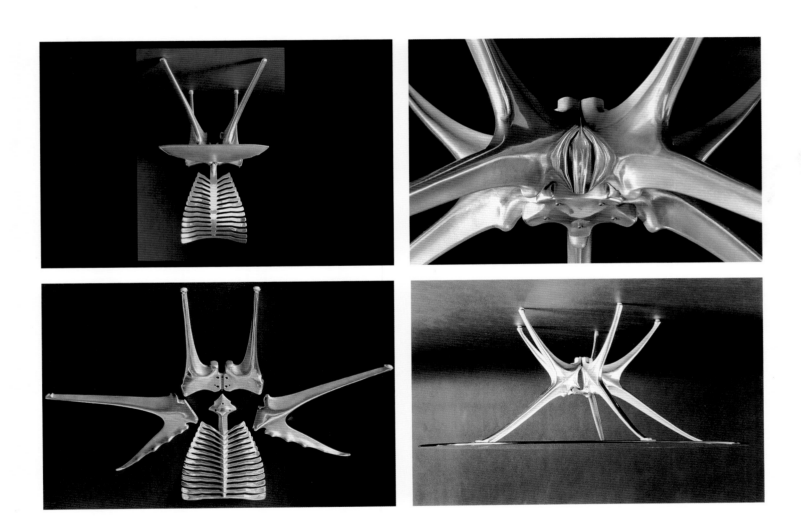

LINDA MAI

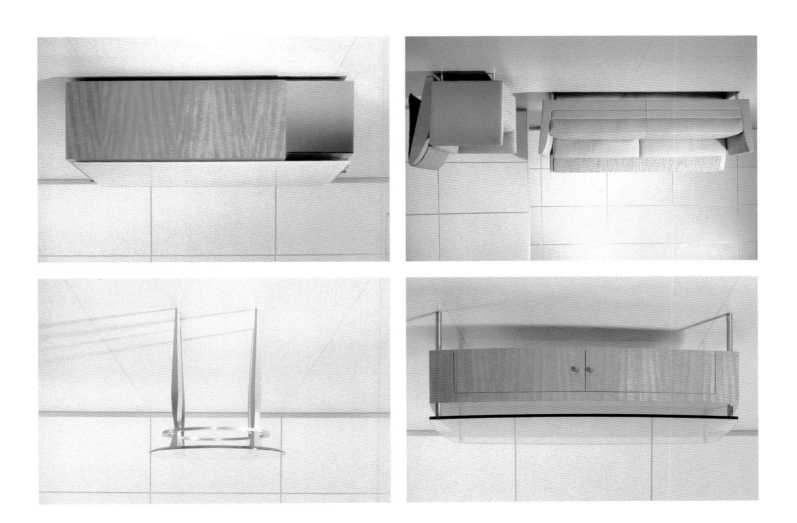

FURNITURE

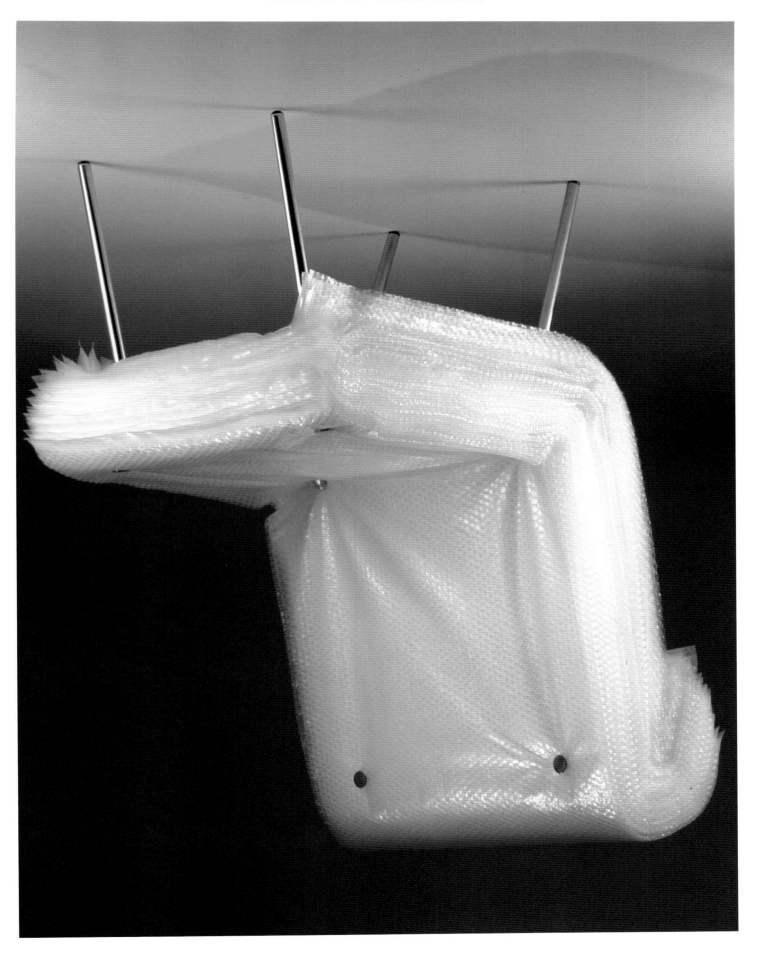

MARCEL WANDERS

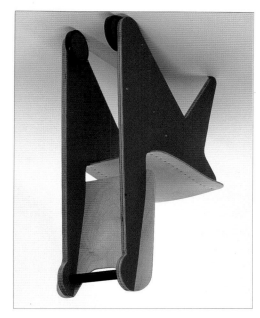

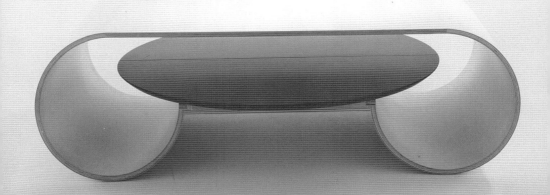

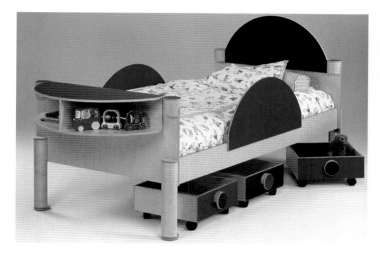

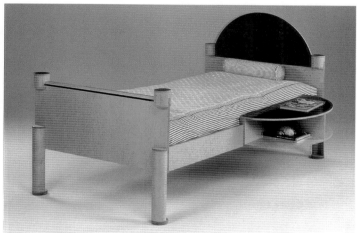

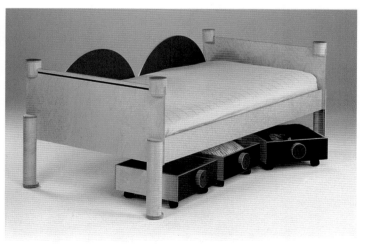

KIDS' STUDIO (IN-HOUSE)

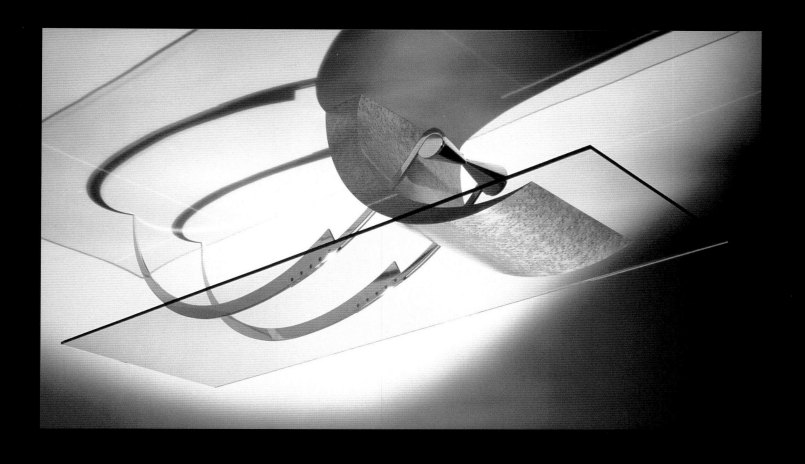

(This spread) **DANIEL TAYLOR & ASSOCIATES (IN-HOUSE)**

WAGNER MURRAY ARCHITECTS (IN-HOUSE)

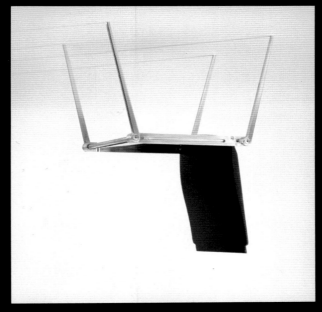

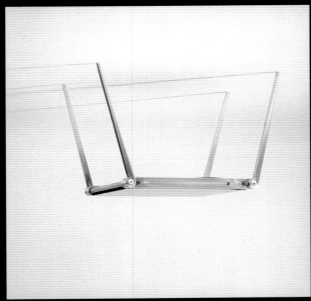

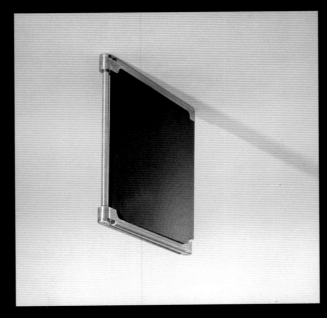

ARSENIO GARCIA-MONSALVE

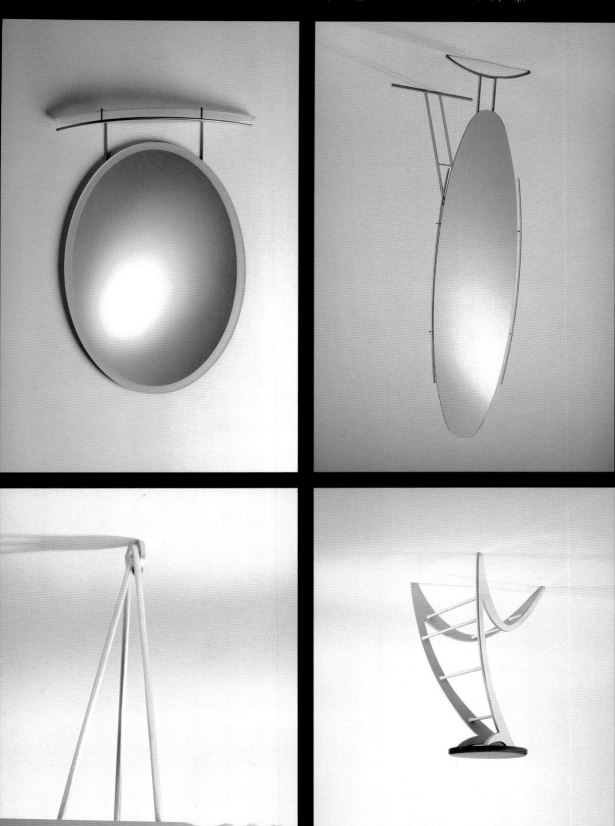

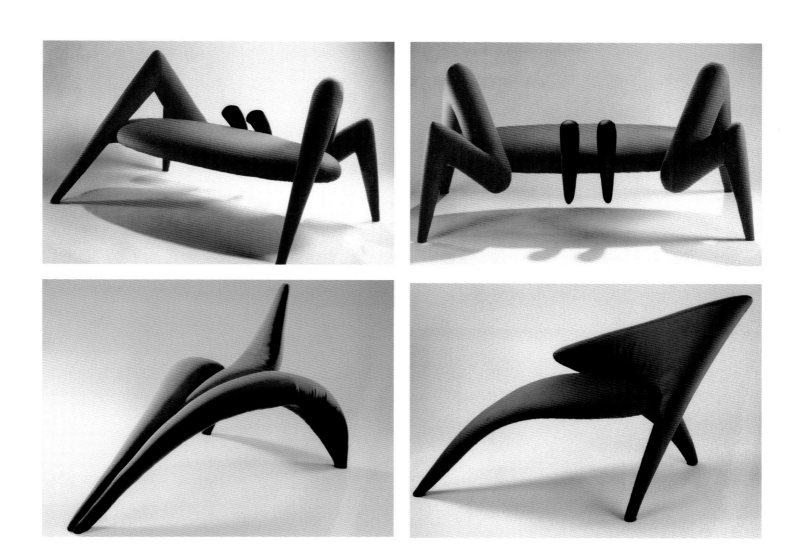

EFI BENBASSA DESIGN STUDIO (IN-HOUSE)

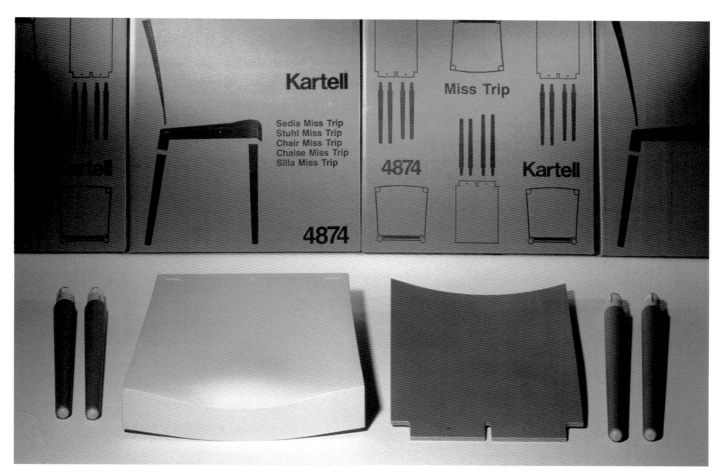

(This spread) **PHILIPPE STARCK** *Kartell*

FURNITURE

KING SIZE (IN-HOUSE)

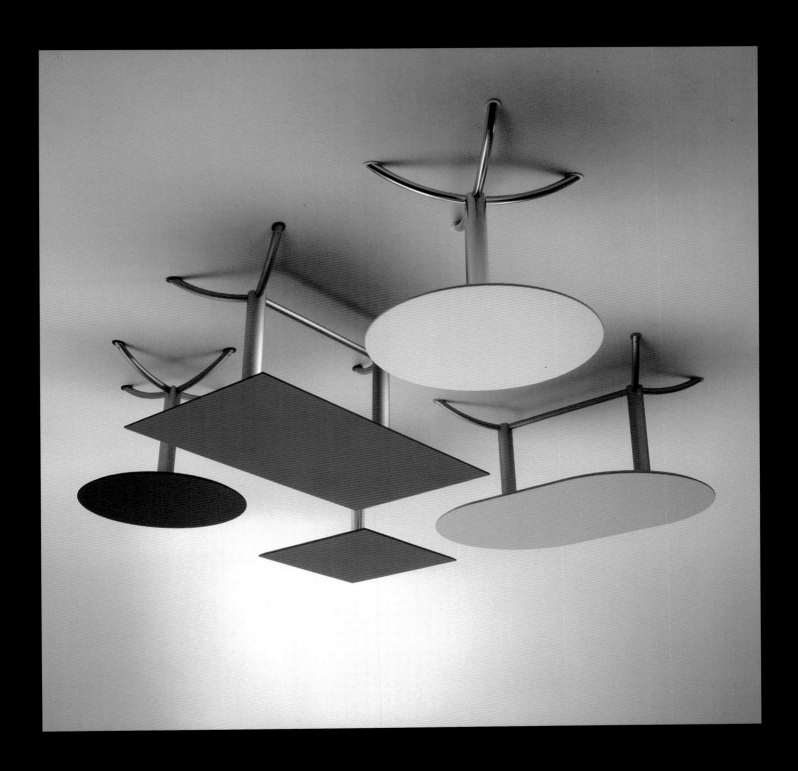

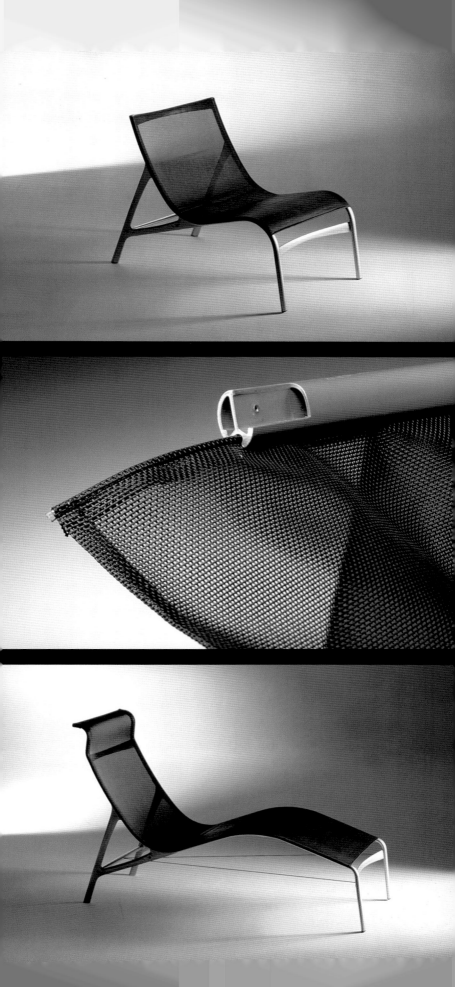

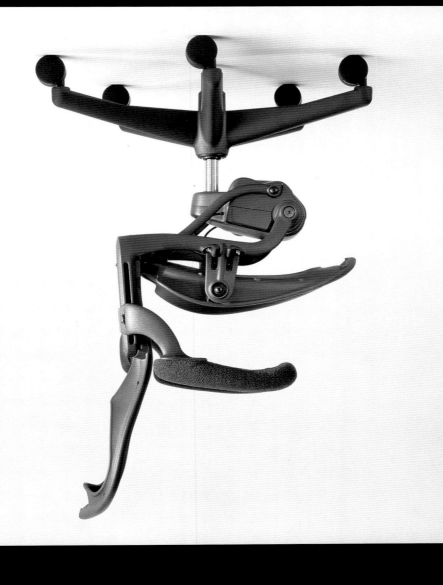

ALTERNATIV STUDIO (IN-HOUSE)

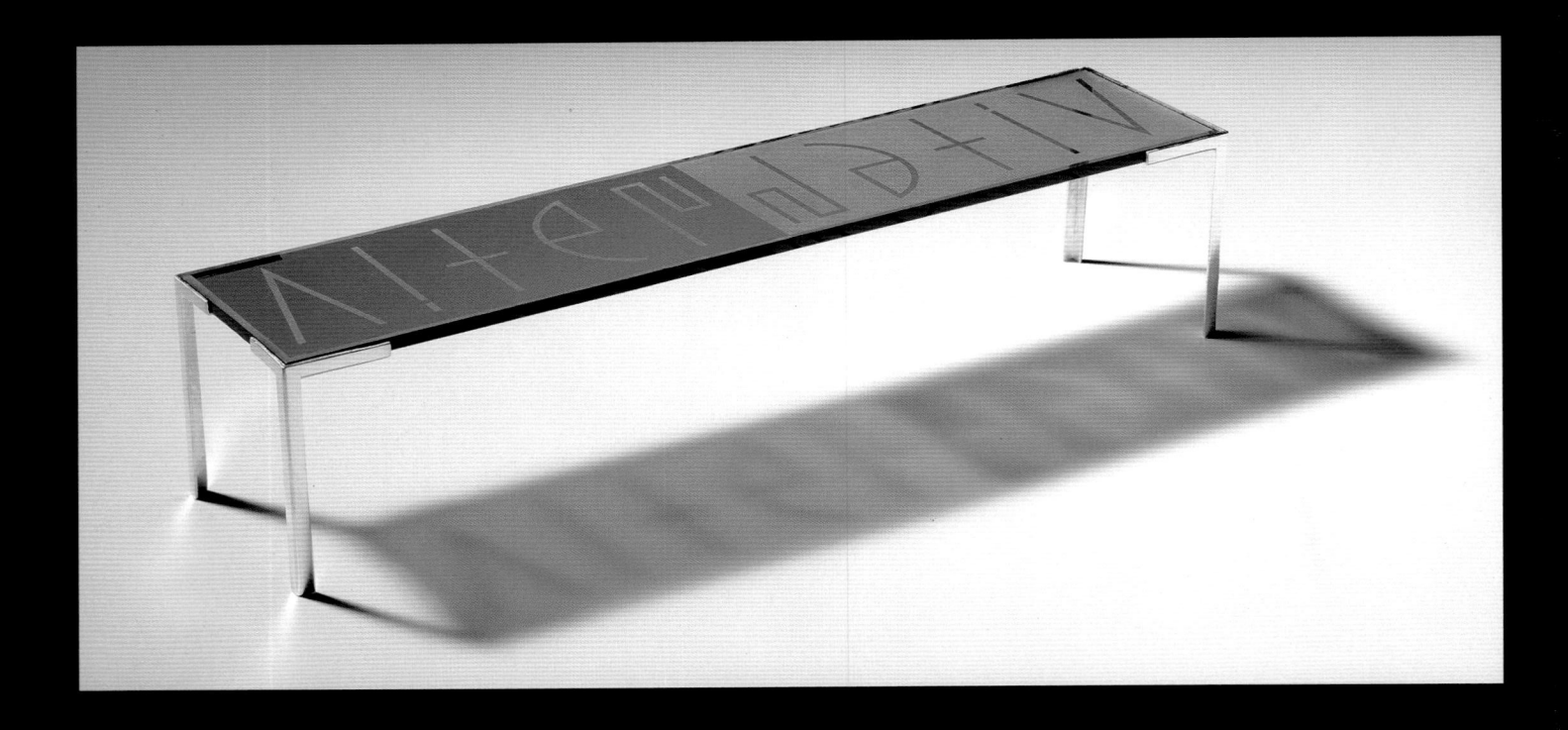

ALTERNATIV STUDIO (IN-HOUSE)

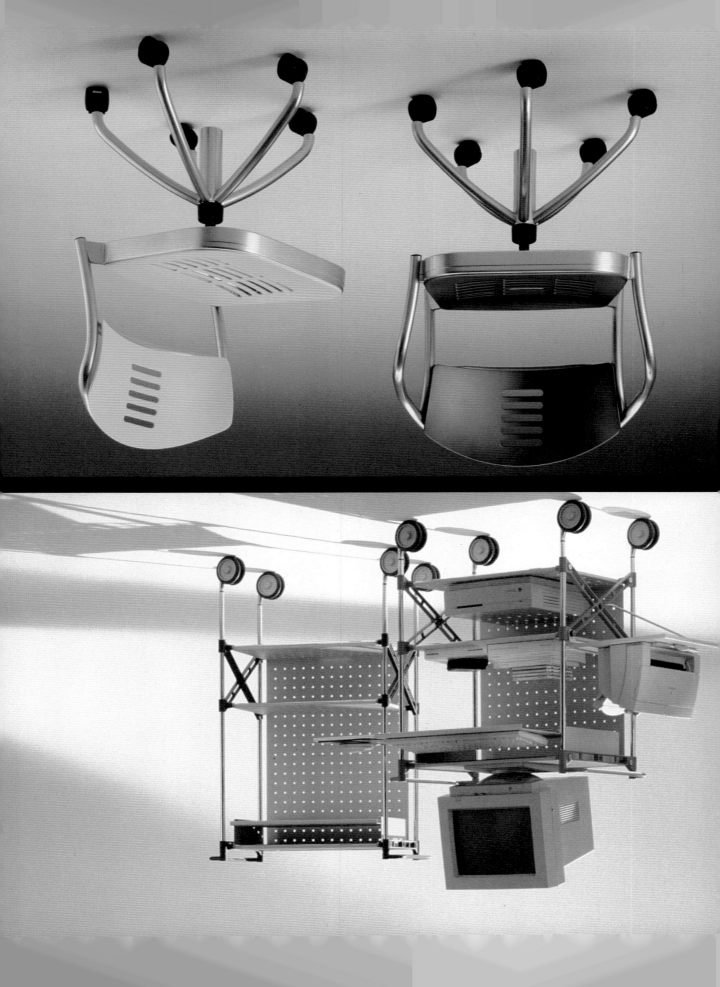

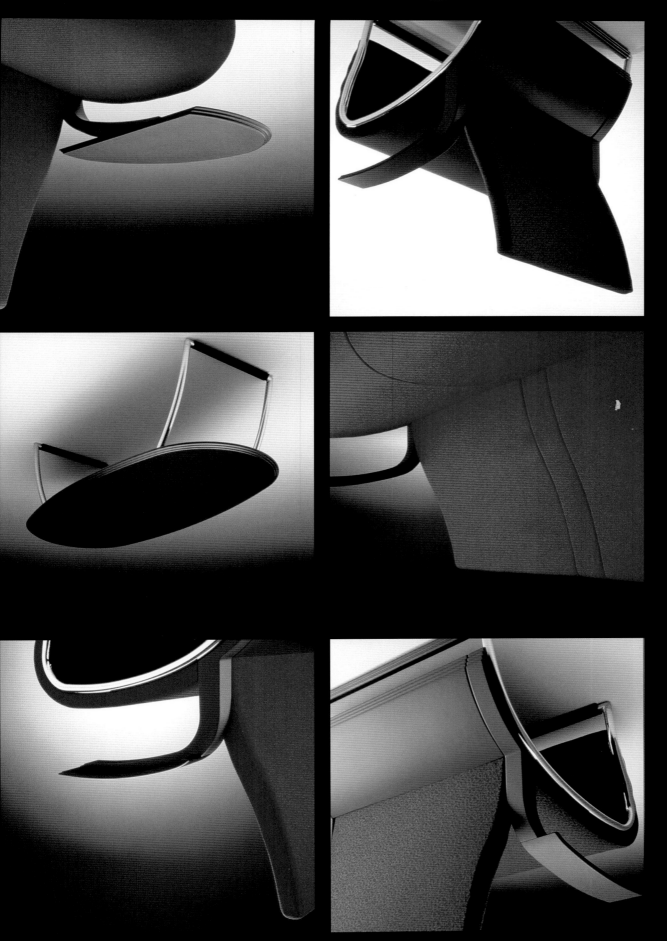

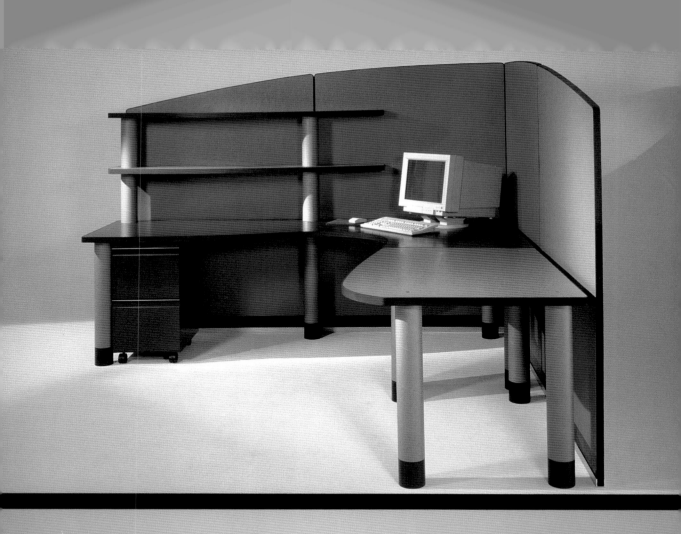

(*This spread*) **THE BURDICK GROUP** *Itoki Co., Ltd.*

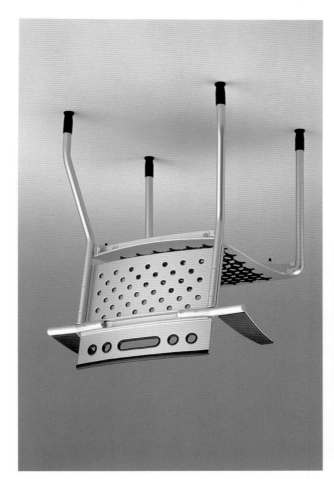

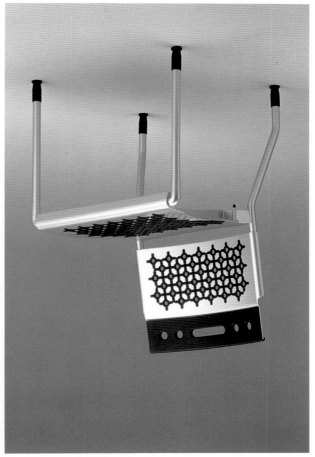

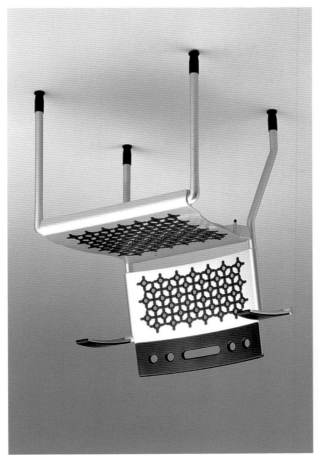

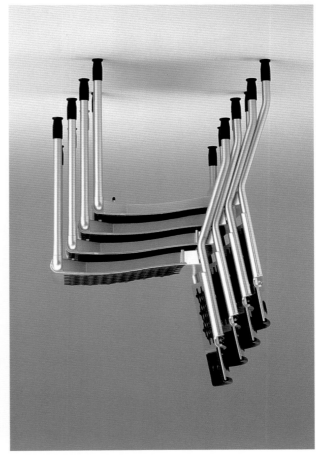

(*This spread*) **THE BURDICK GROUP** *Itoki Co., Ltd.*

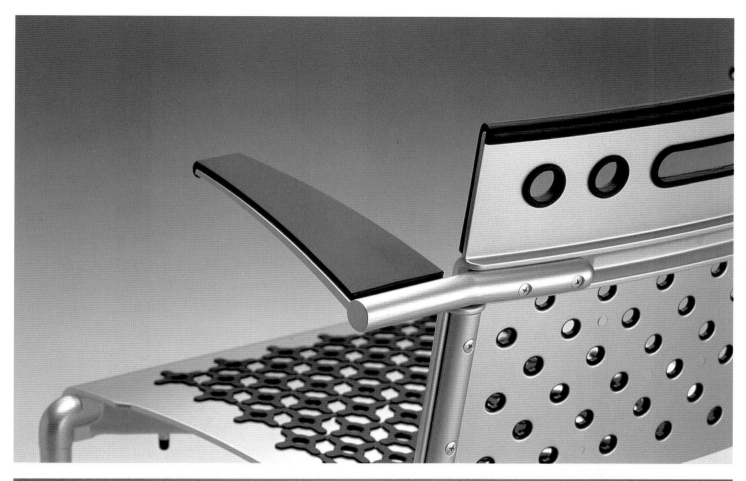

(This spread) THOMAS J. NEWHOUSE DESIGN Herman Miller SQA

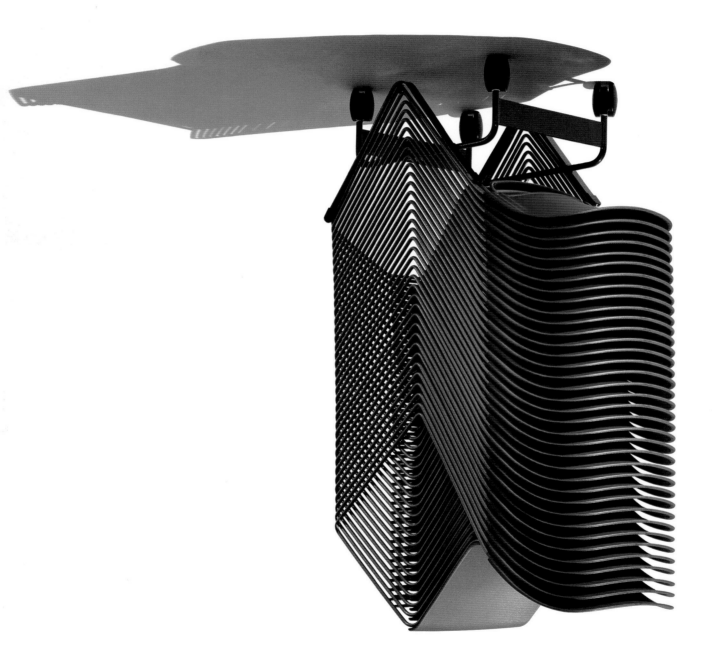

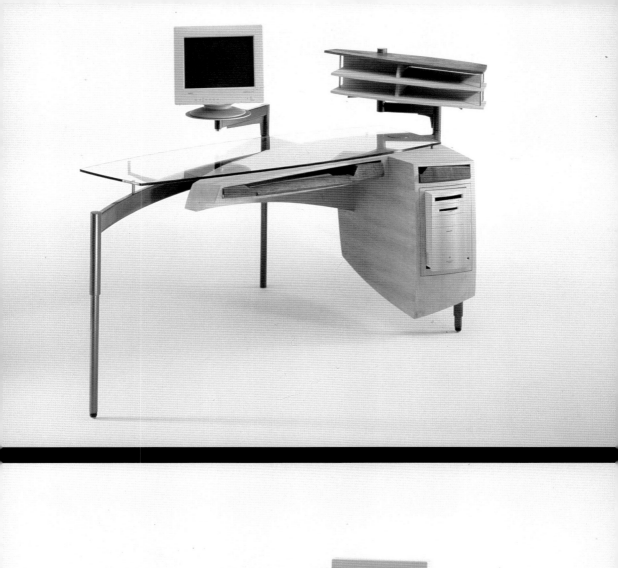

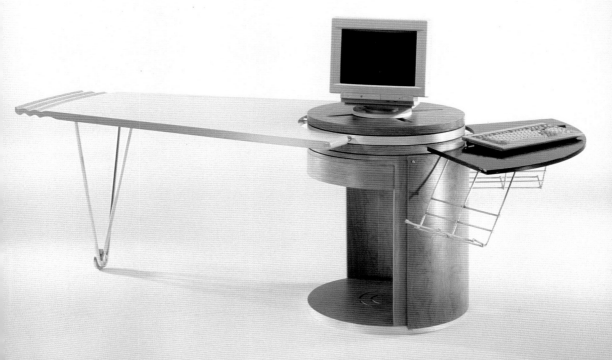

KI (IN-HOUSE)

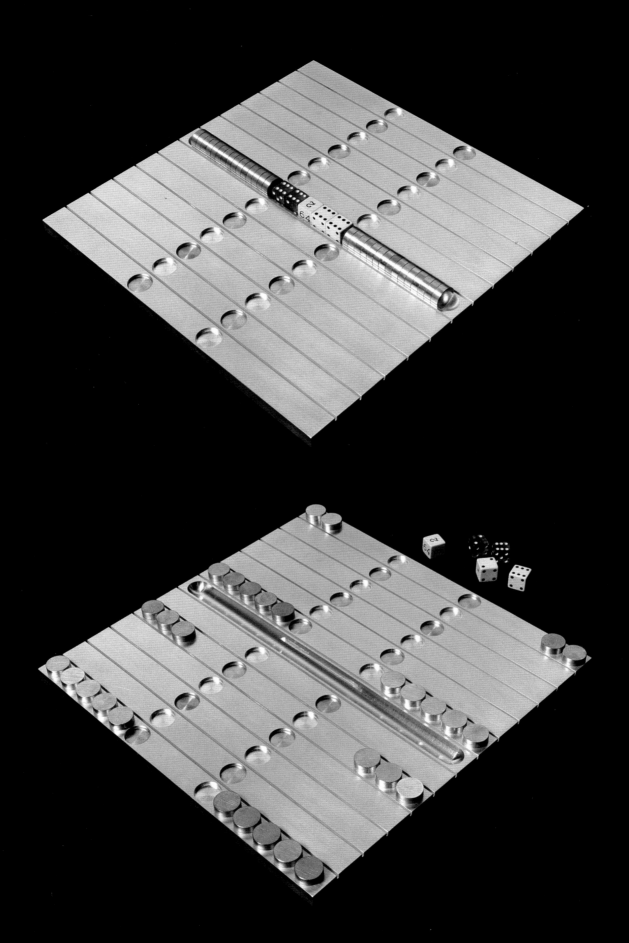

(Opposite page) **MICROSOFT HARDWARE DESIGN GROUP** *Microsoft Corporation* ■ *(This page)* **WAGNER MURRAY ARCHITECTS (IN-HOUSE)**

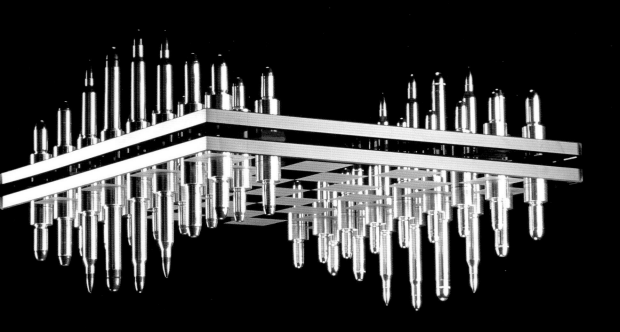

(Top) **SMART DESIGN, INC.** *ALPS Electric USA Inc.* ■ *(Bottom)* **KARO DESIGN RESOURCES INC.** *Advanced Gravis Computer Technology Ltd.*

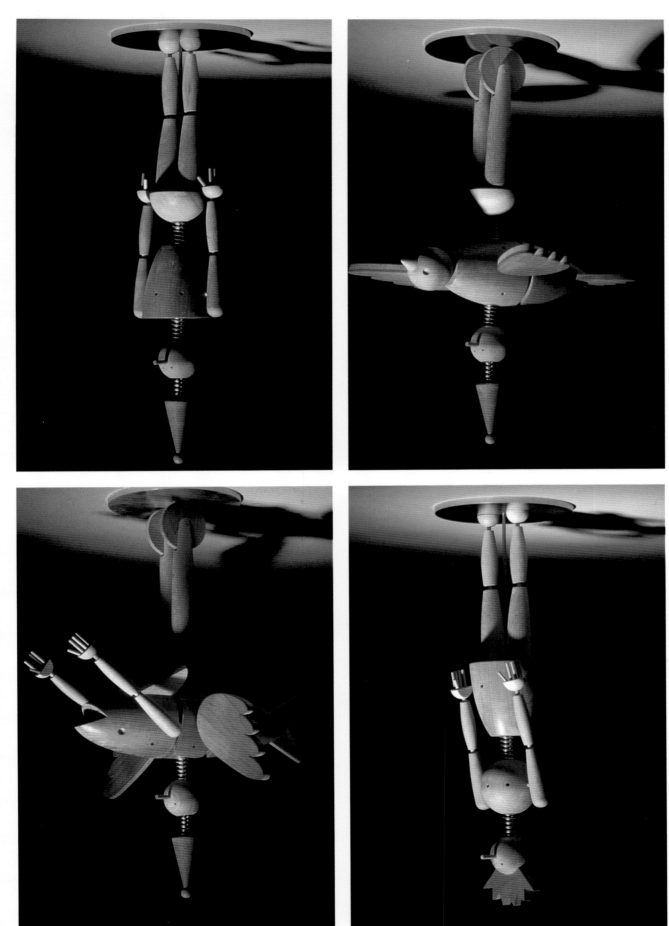

SPORE (IN-HOUSE)

SMART DESIGN, INC. *Oxo International*

ECCO DESIGN, INC. *Recreware*

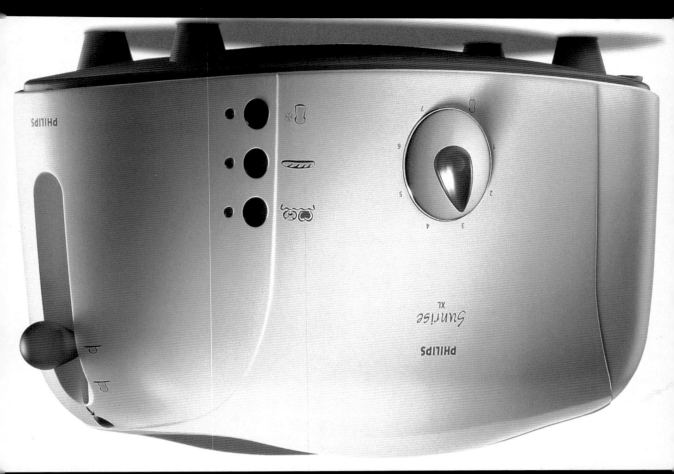

LUNAR DESIGN (IN-HOUSE)

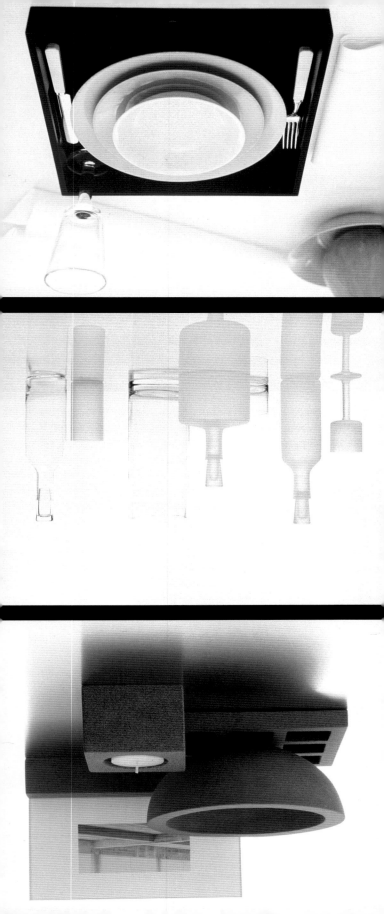

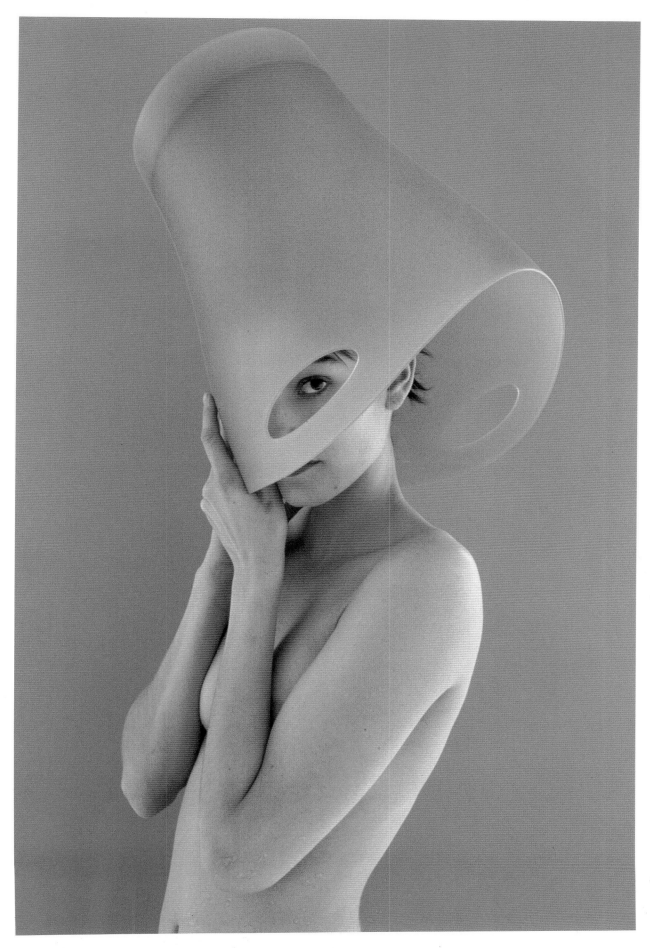

BEYOND DESIGN INC. (IN-HOUSE)

(This spread) **TUPPERWARE (IN-HOUSE)**

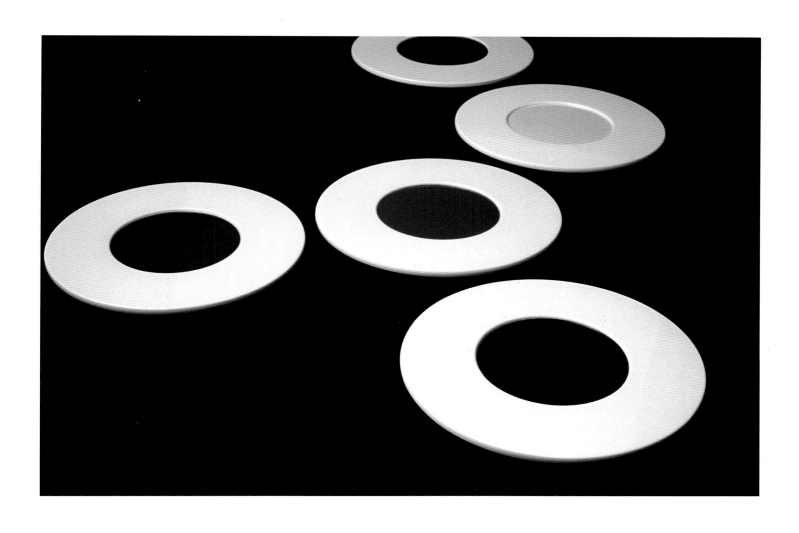

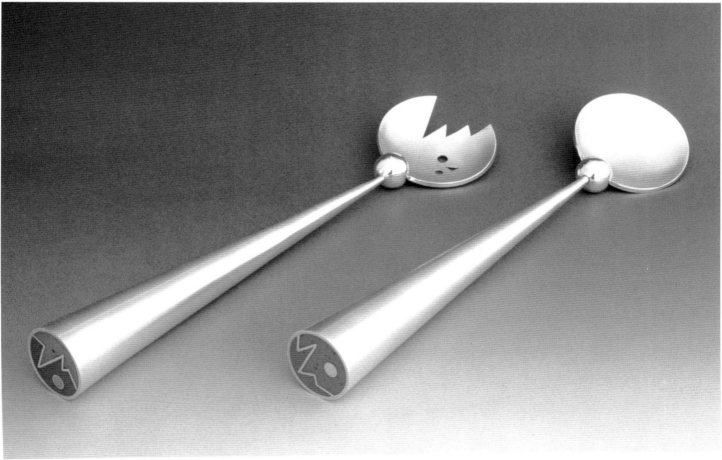

(Top) **TUPPERWARE (IN-HOUSE)** ■ *(Bottom)* **MACBAIN ART METAL (IN-HOUSE)**

(*This spread*) KARIM RASHID INDUSTRIAL DESIGN (IN-HOUSE)

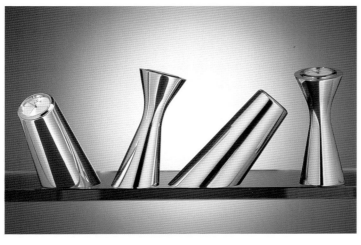

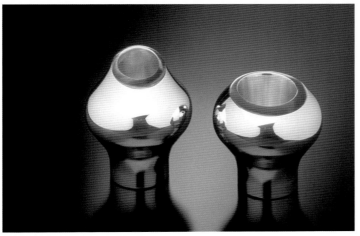

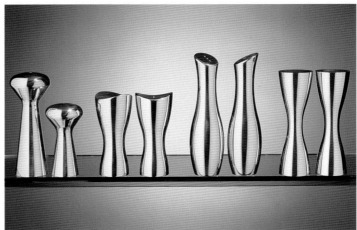

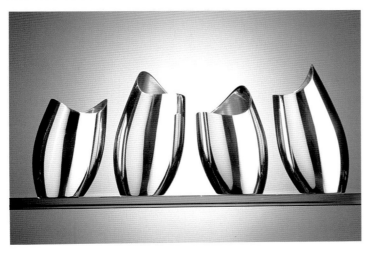

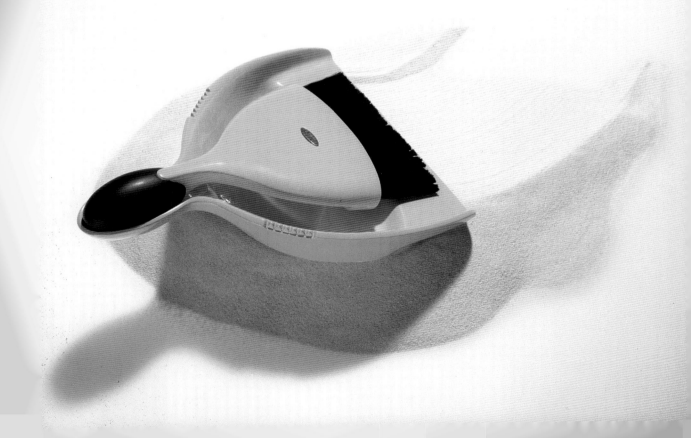

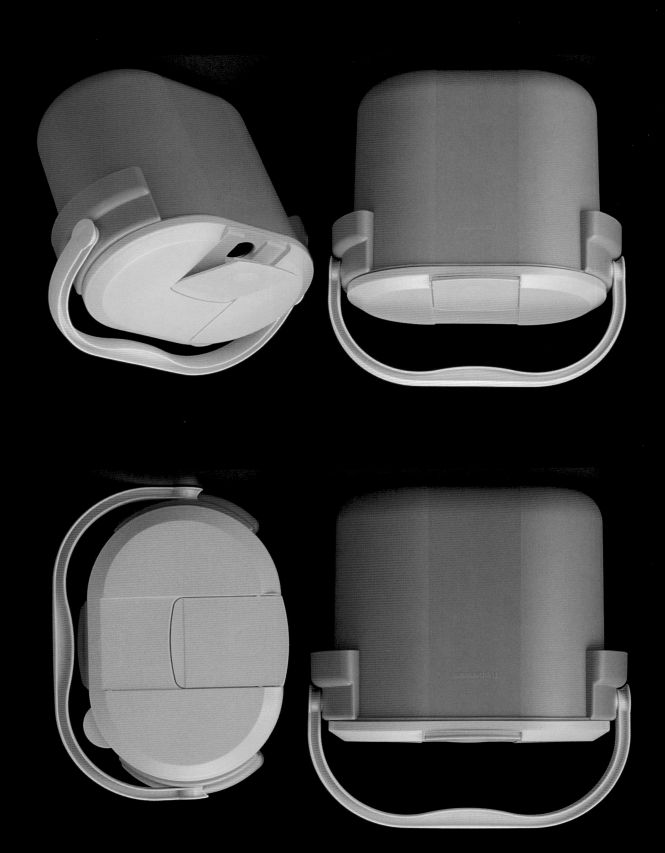

(Top) **ZIBA DESIGN** *Youth Plastic Works* ■ *(Bottom)* **PRODUCT INSIGHT INC.** *Tucker Housewares*

(Top left, bottom left, bottom right) DESIGN CENTRAL GE Appliances Europe ■ (Top right) ROUDEBUSH DESIGN ASSOCIATES Jenn-Air Corporation

TUPPERWARE (IN-HOUSE)

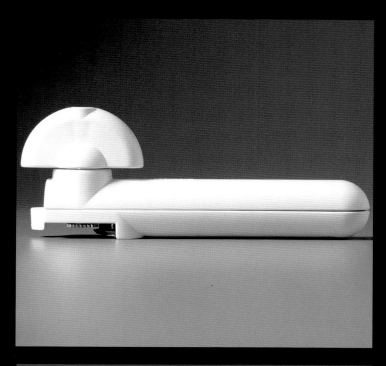

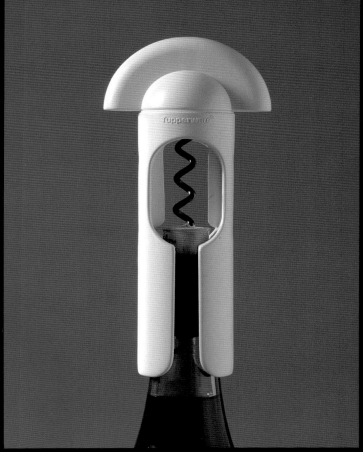

TUPPERWARE (IN-HOUSE)

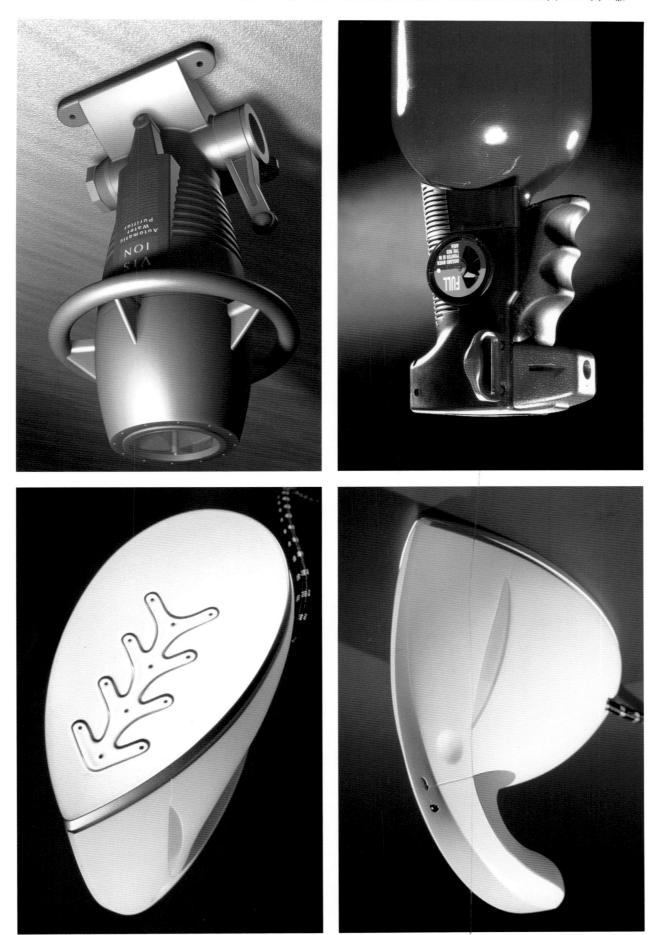

(Top left, top right) IDEO PRODUCT DEVELOPMENT *Matsushita* ∎ (Bottom left) PRODUCT GENESIS, INC. *First Alert*
∎ (Bottom right) PRODUCT GENESIS, INC. *Fountainhead Technologies, Inc.*

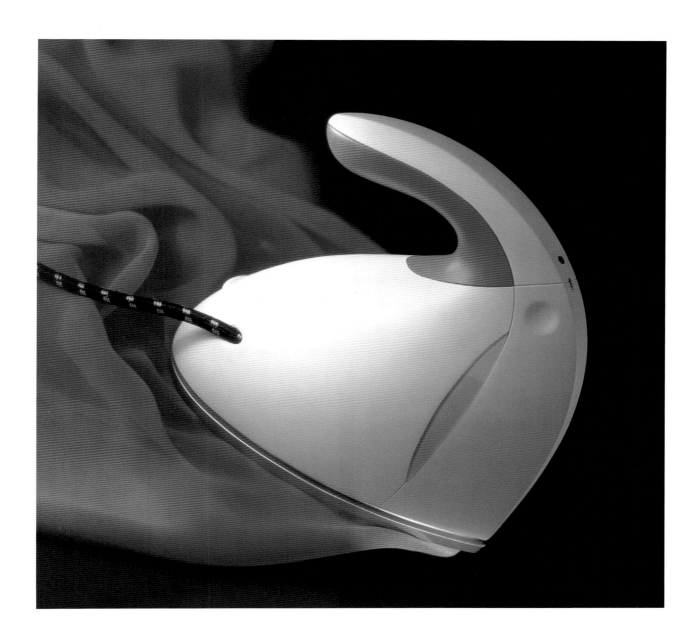

IDEO PRODUCT DEVELOPMENT *Matsushita*

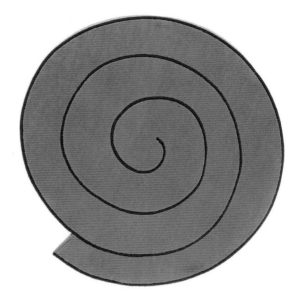

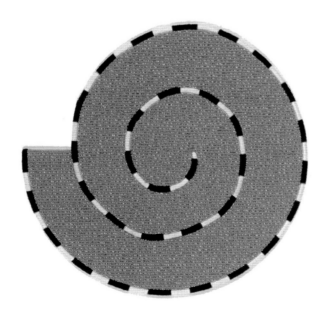

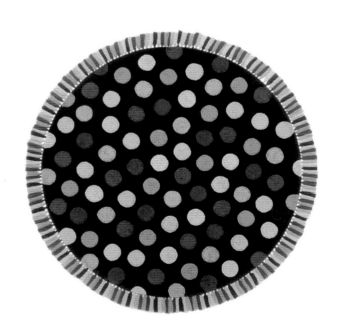

CHRISTINE VAN DER HURD, INC. (IN-HOUSE)

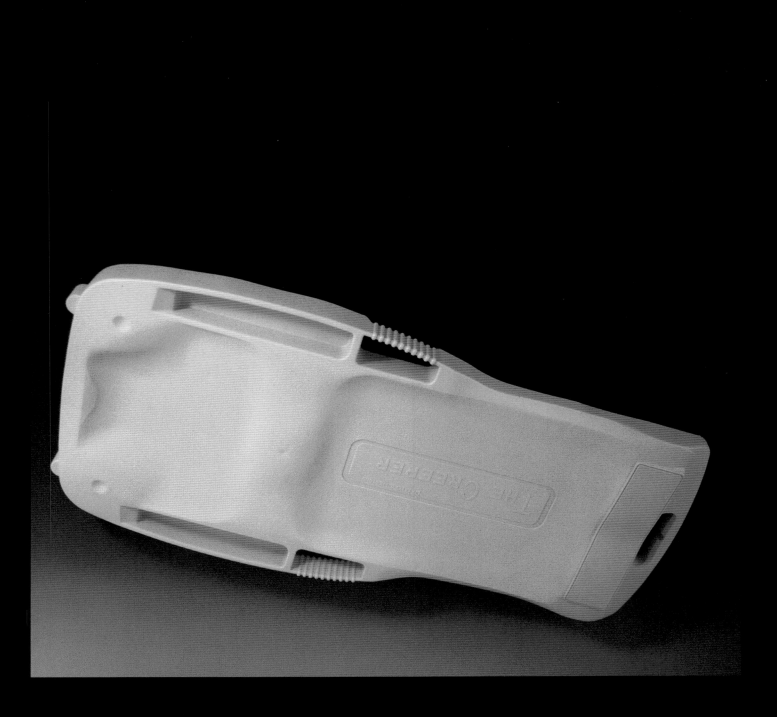

KARO DESIGN RESOURCES INC. *Winsire Enterprises Corporation*

(Top) **GROUP FOUR DESIGN** *Ingersoll-Rand* ■ (Middle) **INTERFORM** *Simple Solutions*
■ (Bottom) **BALLY DESIGN INC.** *Applied Concepts*

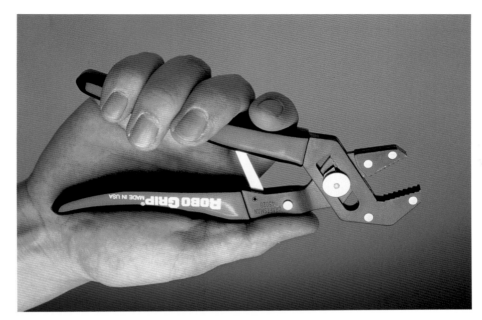

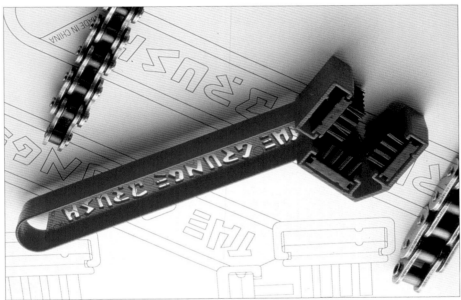

ACME CITY CARTS (IN-HOUSE)

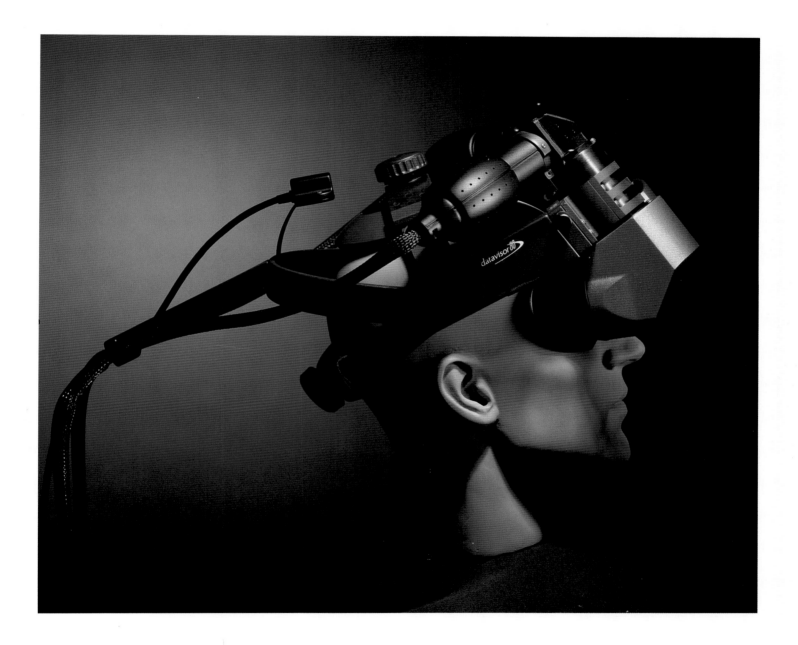

(Opposite page) **LUNAR DESIGN** *Acuson Corporation* ■ *(This page)* **ION DESIGN** *n-Vision*

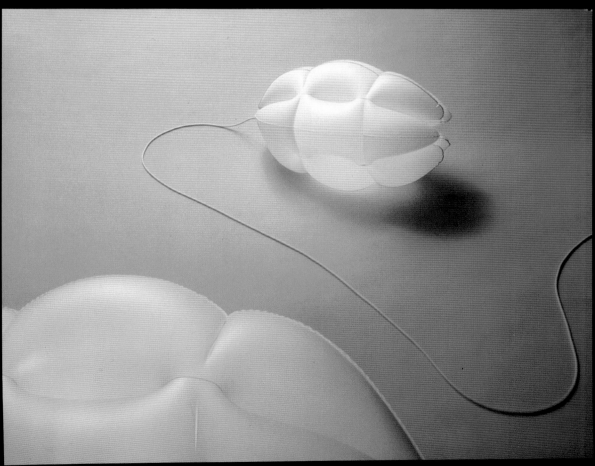

INFLATE (IN-HOUSE)

KROHN DESIGN *Nicola*

HARRY ALLEN & ASSOCIATES (IN-HOUSE)

(Left) **PAULO RIZZATTO** *Luceplan S.p.A.* ■ *(Right)* **DROOG DESIGN (IN-HOUSE)**

(Opposite page) TZ DESIGN, JHANE BARNES, DMJ ROTTET Bernhardt.
■ (Bottom left, bottom right) OFFICE O (IN-HOUSE) ■ LYNCH/FRINTA, ARCHITECTURE/DESIGN (IN-HOUSE)
(Top left, top right)

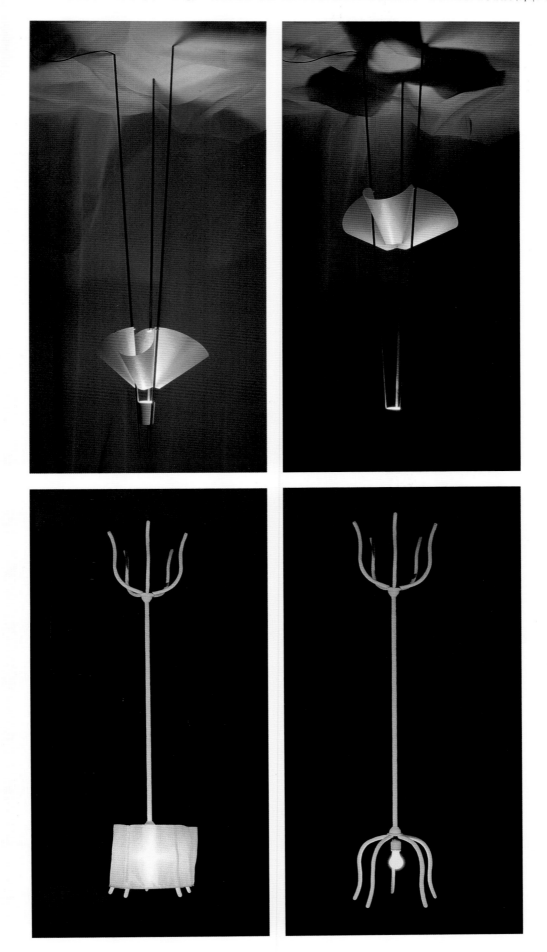

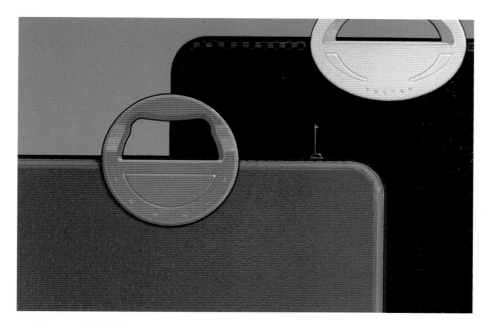

(Top, bottom) **MACHINEART (IN-HOUSE)** ■ *(Middle)* **STUDIO OZ (IN-HOUSE)**

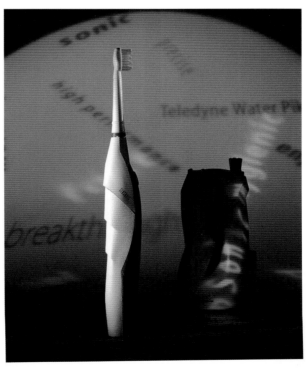

(Opposite page) **DESIGNDESIGN** *Smith & Nephew/Donjoy* ■ *(This page, top)* **SMART DESIGN, INC.** *Johnson & Johnson*
■ *(This page, bottom)* **MACHINEART** *Teledyne Waterpik*

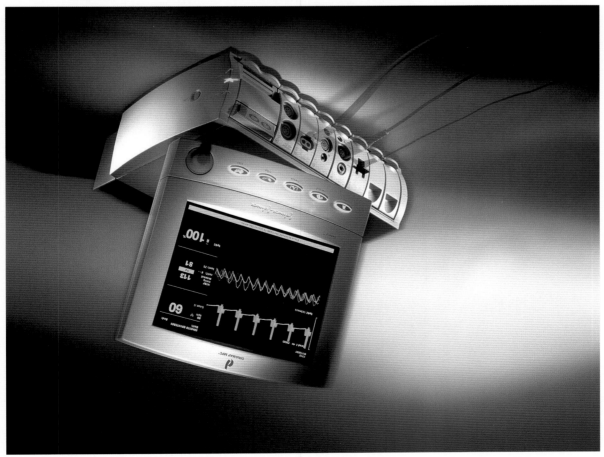

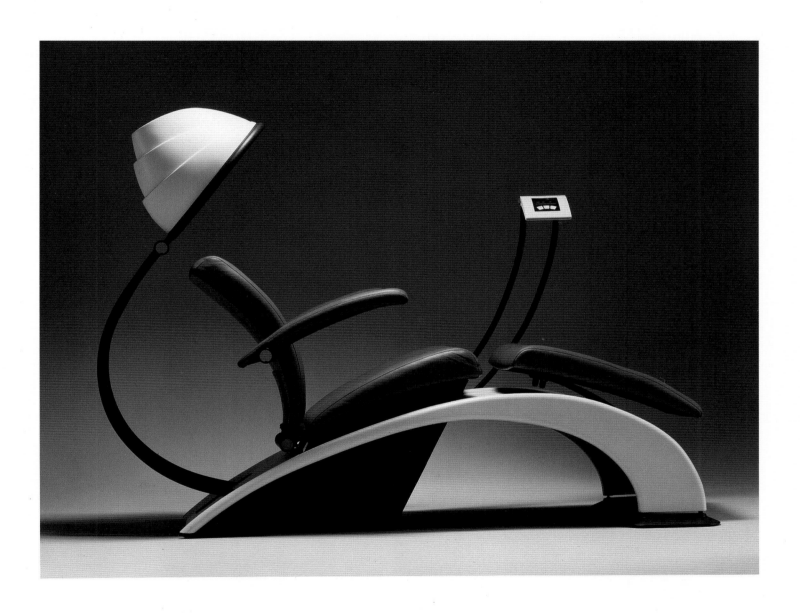

KARO DESIGN RESOURCES INC. *Current Technolgy Corporation*

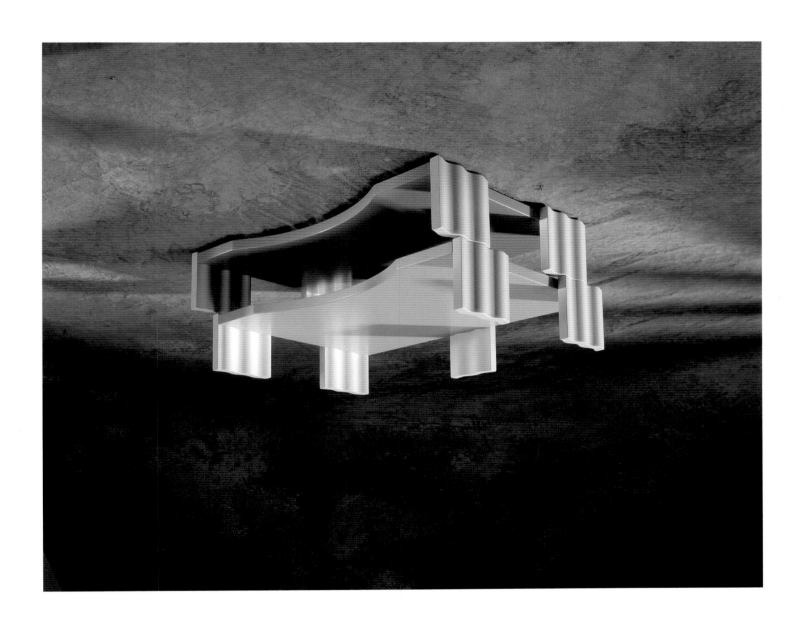

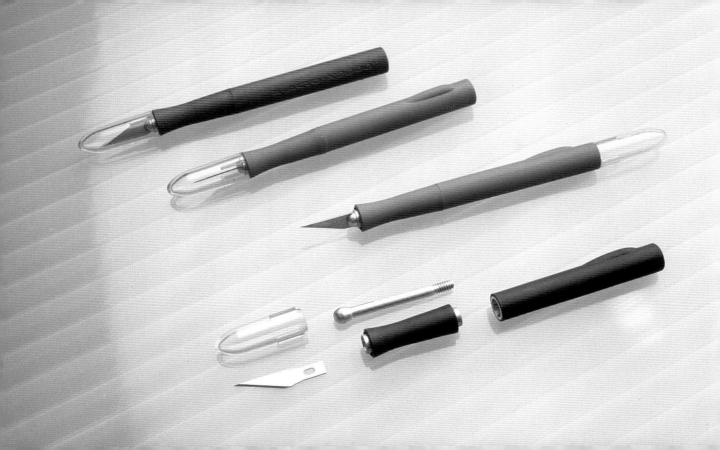

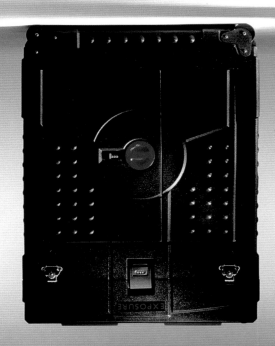

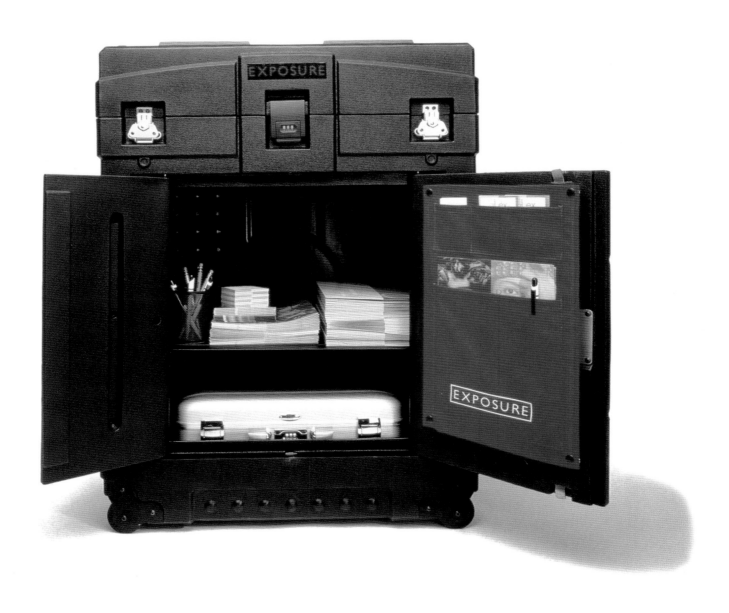

(This spread) **STUART KARTEN DESIGN** *Abex Display Systems*

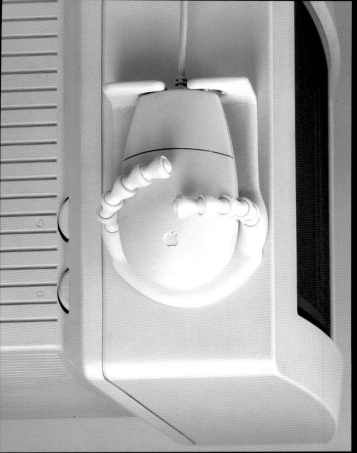

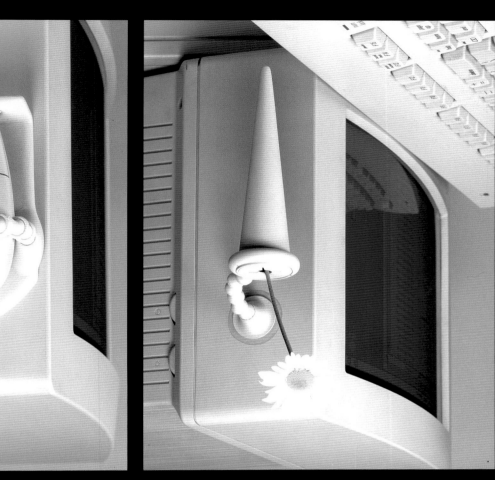

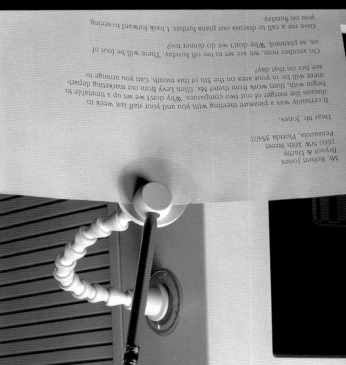

Dear Mr. Jones.

It certainly was a pleasure meeting with you and your staff last week to discuss the merger of our two companies. Why don't we set up a timetable to begin with, then work from there? Ms. Ellen Levy from our marketing department will be in your area on the 5th of this month. Can you arrange to see her on that day?

On another note, we are set to tee off Sunday. There will be four of us, as planned. Why don't we do dinner too?

Give me a call to discuss our plans further. I look forward to seeing you on Sunday.

Mr. Robert Jones
Bryant & Darby
1600 NW 26th Street
Pensacola, Florida 35401

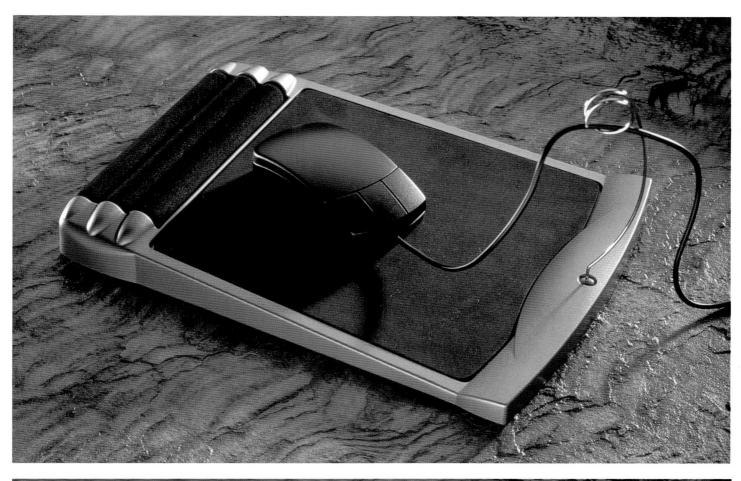

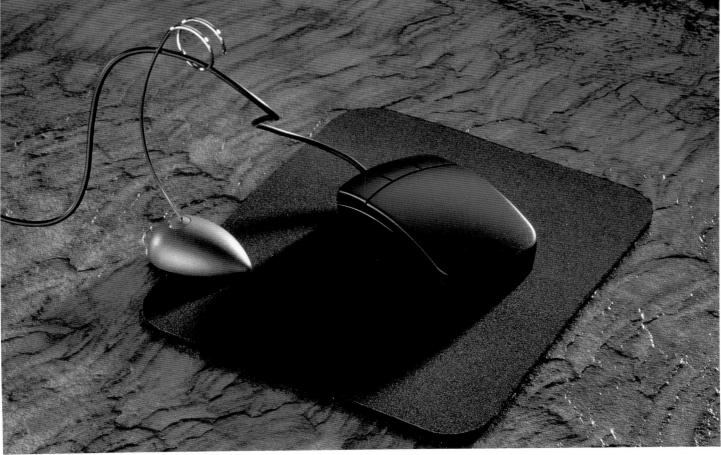

EXO DESIGN *Pantech International*

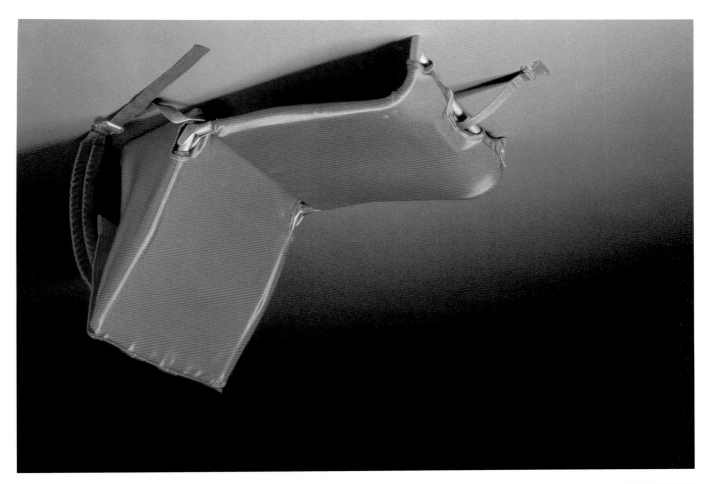

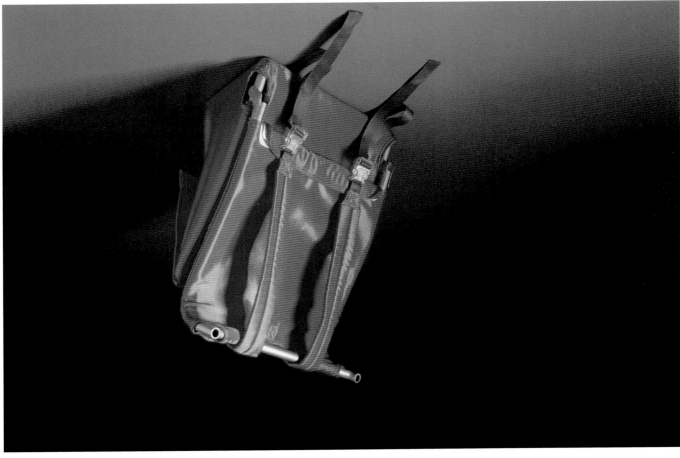

(Top) **DESIGN WORKSHOP** *Safe Cycle* ■ *(Bottom)* **DESIGNWORKS/USA** *Scott*

(Top) **DESIGNWORKS/USA** *Fichtel & Sachs AG* ■ *(Bottom)* **DESIGNWORKS/USA** *Scott*

(Top) **SIMON & GOETZ** *adp engineering GmbH* ▪ *(Bottom)* **FRIDOLIN BEISERT, MICHAEL SANS**

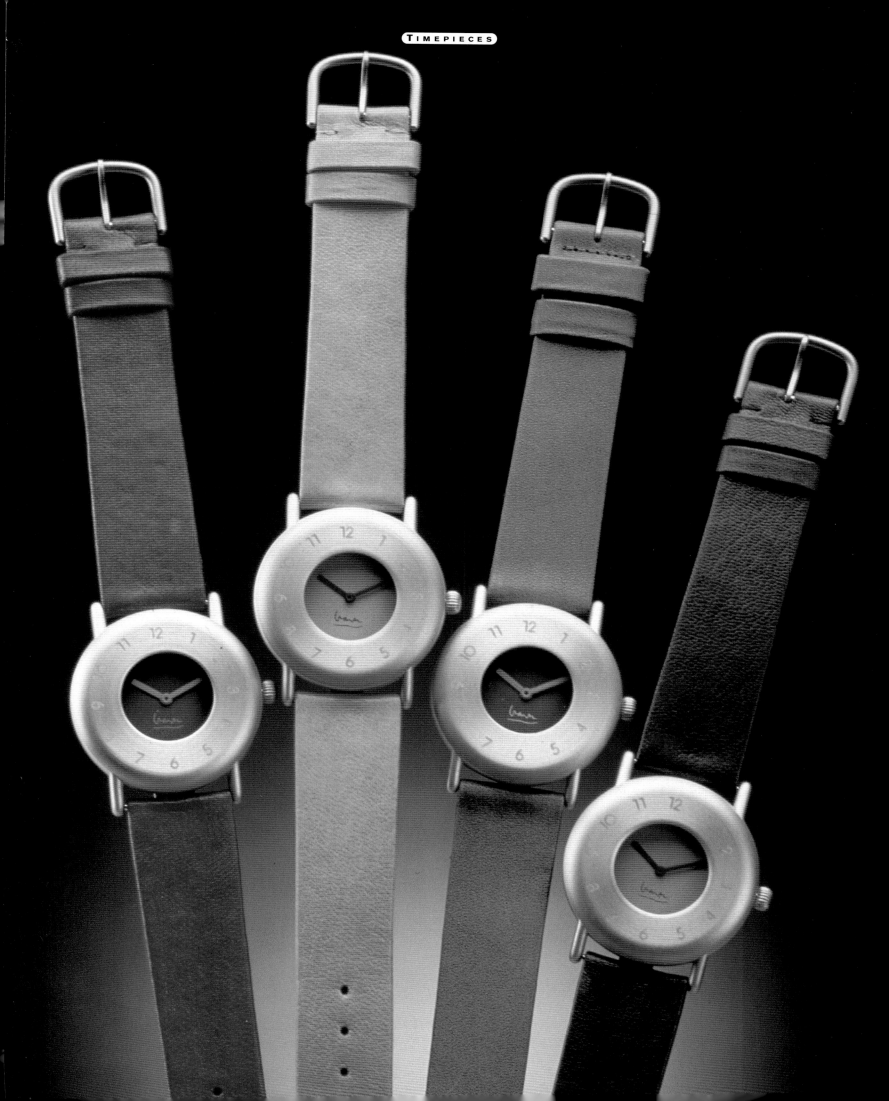

(Top) **GRAVES DESIGN** *The Martuse Corporation* ■ (Bottom) **BOD DESIGN** (IN-HOUSE)

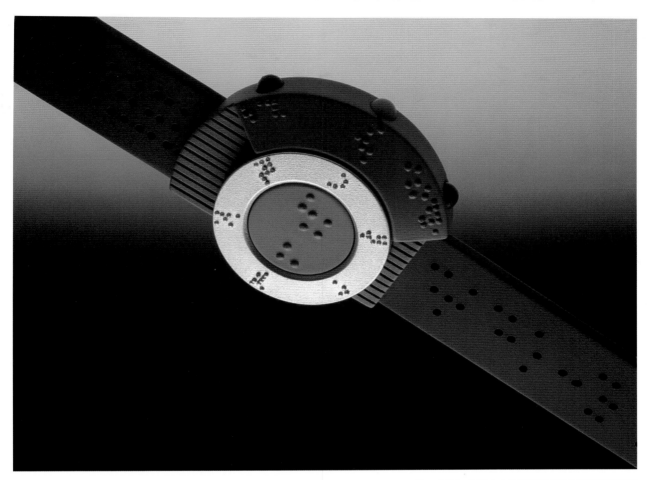

(Top) **SIGMAG (IN-HOUSE)** ■ *(Bottom)* **CKS PARTNERS** *Pixar Animation Studios*

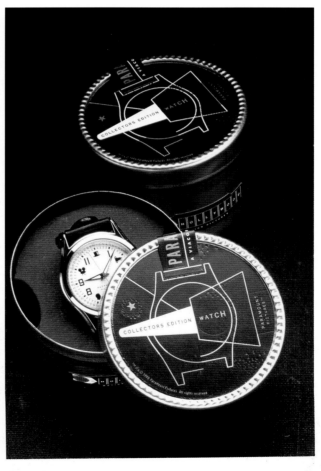

(Top left, top right) **SMART DESIGN** *Timex, Joe Boxer* ■ *(Bottom left, bottom right)* **CHARLES S. ANDERSON DESIGN** *Paramount/Fujisankei*

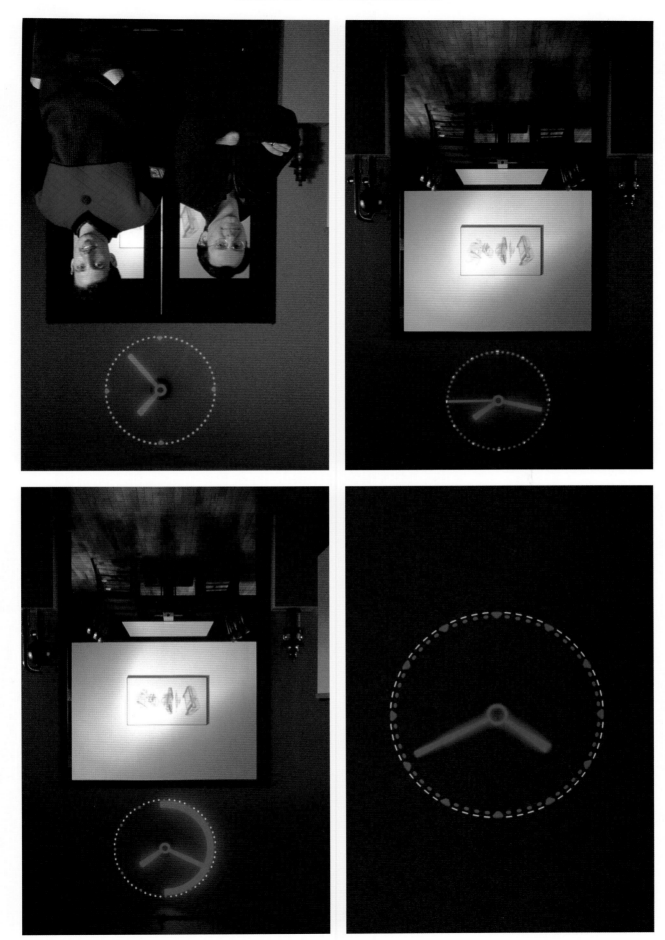

ALAN CHAN DESIGN COMPANY *Alan Chan Creations*

 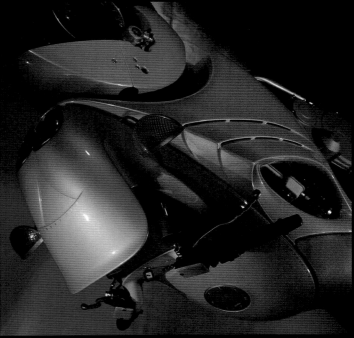

(*Top*) STUDIO MARTONE (IN-HOUSE) ■ (*Bottom*) BMW AG (IN-HOUSE)

TRANSPORTATION

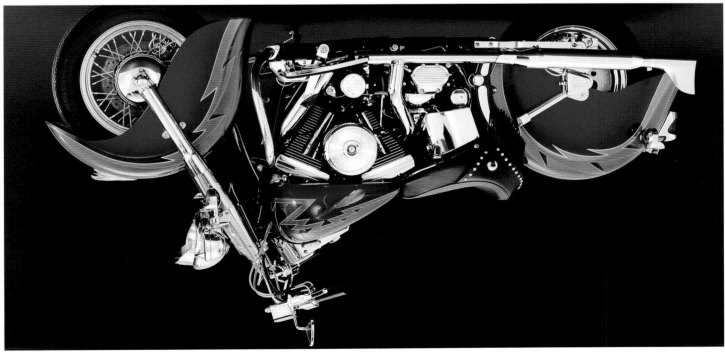

TRANSPORTATION

CAPTIONS AND CREDITS

LEGENDEN UND KUNSTLERANGABEN

LEGENDES ET ARTISTES

PAGES 14, 15 PRODUCT: *Polaroid Portable Digital Camera Compact Disc DCCD Still Video & Audio Recorder* DESIGN FIRM: *Polaroid Design Center* DESIGNER: *Peter Rolicki* PRODUCT PHOTOGRAPHER: *Tony Rinaldo* MANUFACTURER: *Polaroid Corporation* MATERIALS: *ABS* DESIGN DATE: *5/94*

PAGES 16, 17 PRODUCT: *Digital Image/Sound/Pen Input & Output Device* DESIGN FIRM: *Design Edge* DESIGNER: *Mark S. Kimbrough* PRODUCT PHOTOGRAPHER: *Stence & Stence* MANUFACTURER: *Edgeworks* MATERIALS: *ABS* DESIGN DATE: *9/95* PRODUCTION DATE: *4/96*

PAGES 18, 19 PRODUCT: *CD Player and Boom Box* DESIGN FIRM: *IDEO Product Development* DESIGNER: *Richard Salinas* PRODUCT PHOTOGRAPHER: *Steve Moeder, IDEO Product Development* MANUFACTURER: *Galaxy Brands* MATERIALS: *Injection-molded ABS* DESIGN DATE: *11/96*

PAGES 20, 21 PRODUCT: *Jeep Portable Stereo Unit* DESIGN FIRM: *Human Factors Industrial Design Inc.* DESIGNERS: *Skip Kirk, Paul Lacotta, Walter Stoeckmann* PRODUCT PHOTOGRAPHER: *John Moldauer, Human Factors Industrial Design Inc.* MANUFACTURER: *Kash n' Gold* MATERIALS: *Injection-molded ABS, Acetel, PP* DESIGN YEAR: *1994* PRODUCTION YEAR: *1995* LAUNCH YEAR: *1995*

PAGE 22 (TOP) PRODUCT: *Monitor* DESIGN FIRM: *Void* DESIGNER: *Thomas Meyerhoffer* PRODUCT PHOTOGRAPHER: *Rick English, Rick English Pictures* CLIENT: *NEC Electronics* MANUFACTURER: *NEC Electronics* DESIGN YEAR: *1995* PRODUCTION DATE: *1/96* LAUNCH DATE: *3/96*

PAGE 22 (BOTTOM) PRODUCT: *Monitor* DESIGN FIRM: *IDEO Product Development* DESIGNER: *Jochen Backs* PRODUCT PHOTOGRAPHER: *Steve Moeder, IDEO Product Development* MANUFACTURER: *Samsung Electronics* MATERIALS: *Injection-molded ABS* LAUNCH DATE: *1/97*

PAGE 23 PRODUCT: *Laser Printer* DESIGN FIRM: *Kasom Design* DESIGNERS: *Wayne Kasom, Clare Johnson* PRODUCT PHOTOGRAPHER: *Henrik Kam, Henrik Kam Photography, Inc.* MANUFACTURER: *Powis Parker Company* MATERIALS: *Structural Foam, Aluminum, ABS* DESIGN YEAR: *1995* PRODUCTION DATE: *1/96* LAUNCH DATE: *1/96*

PAGE 24 PRODUCT: *Alpha Server 4100, 800, 500 Personal Workstation* DESIGN FIRM: *Digital Equipment Corporation* DESIGNERS: *Robert Hanson, Bernard Maurer, and Richard Johnson of Digital Equipment Corporation and Scott Stropkay, Leif Huff, Mark Nichols of IDEO Product Development* PRODUCT PHOTOGRAPHER: *Monty Abbott, Monty Abbott Photography* MANUFACTURER: *Digital Equipment Corporation* MATERIALS: *Injection-molded ABS, steel, polycarbonate* DESIGN DATE: *2/96* PRODUCTION DATE: *12/96* LAUNCH DATE: *12/96*

PAGE 25 PRODUCT: *Impactdata NPA (Network Peripheral Adapter)* DESIGN FIRM: *Ashcraft Design* ART DIRECTOR: *Daniel Ashcraft* DESIGNER: *Trung Phung* PRODUCT PHOTOGRAPHERS: *Tony Garcia, Donald Miller* MANUFACTURER: *Impactdata* DESIGN DATE: *9/96* PRODUCTION DATE: *5/97* LAUNCH DATE: *10/96*

PAGES 26, 27 PRODUCT: *AS/400 Advanced Series Computer* DESIGN FIRM: *IBM Corporation* DESIGNERS: *Tim K. Murphy, David Hill* PRODUCT PHOTOGRAPHER: *Bill Diers, Greer & Associates* MANUFACTURER: *IBM Corporation* MATERIALS: *Preplated steel, polycarbonate ABS* DESIGN YEARS: *1993-1994* PRODUCTION DATE: *5/94* LAUNCH DATE: *5/94*

PAGE 28 PRODUCT: *PET (Personal Enhancement Tool)* DESIGN FIRM: *Pi Design* DESIGNER: *Hector Santos* PRODUCT PHOTOGRAPHER: *Randy Highlight Graphics* CLIENT: *Climax ITG* MATERIALS: *ABS, stainless steel* DESIGN DATE: *4/96*

PAGE 29 PRODUCT: *Cymax Color Printer* DESIGN FIRM: *Hauser, Inc.* ART DIRECTOR: *Ron Pierce* DESIGNER: *Davis Weir* PRODUCT PHOTOGRAPHER: *Terry Sutherland, Sutherland Photo Design* CLIENT: *Datametrics Corporation* MATERIALS: *Thermoformed ABS, steel, die-cast aluminum* DESIGN DATE: *10/94* PRODUCTION DATE: *6/95* LAUNCH DATE: *6/95*

PAGE 30 PRODUCT: *Personal Computer System* DESIGN FIRM: *frogdesign, inc.* MANUFACTURER: *Acer American Corporation* MATERIALS: *Recyclable parts, sheet metal, metallic paint* LAUNCH YEAR: *1995*

PAGE 31 PRODUCT: *Liquidvision Peripherals and Keyboard* DESIGN FIRM: *designDESIGN* MANUFACTURER/CLIENT: *Comstream* MATERIALS: *ABS* DESIGN DATE: *3/97* PRODUCTION DATE: *3/97*

PAGES 32, 33 PRODUCT: *Powerbook Laptop Personal Computer* DESIGN FIRM: *Apple Computer Inc.* DESIGNER: *Thomas Meyerhöffer* PRODUCT PHOTOGRAPHER: *Rick English* DESIGN YEAR: *1996* PRODUCTION DATE: *1/97* LAUNCH DATE: *2/97*

PAGE 34 PRODUCT: *Oracle N/C Powerbook Laptop Personal Computer* DESIGN FIRM: *frogdesign, inc.* MANUFACTURER/CLIENT: *Network Computer Inc. (an Oracle Company)* MATERIALS: *cover in rubber, neoprene, leather, plastic, or denim* DESIGN YEAR: *1996*

PAGE 35 PRODUCT: *Enterprise PowerMac* DESIGN FIRM: *frogdesign, inc.* CLIENT: *Macworld* MATERIALS: *injection-molded ABS, fabric/foam, glass* LAUNCH YEAR: *1996*

PAGE 36 PRODUCT: *Galileo New Powerbook* DESIGN FIRM: *frogdesign, inc.* CLIENT: *Macworld* LAUNCH YEAR: *1996*

PAGE 37 PRODUCT: *Oracle N/C (Network Computer)* DESIGN FIRM: *frogdesign, inc.* CLIENT: *Network Computer Inc. (an Oracle Company)*

PAGE 38 PRODUCT: *Clip Fone* DESIGN FIRM: *frogdesign, inc.* PRODUCT PHOTOGRAPHER: *Rick English* CLIENT/MANUFACTURER: *Astralink Technologies*

PAGE 39 PRODUCT: *Jeep Portable Phone* DESIGN FIRM: *Human Factors Industrial Design, Inc.* DESIGNERS: *Skip Kirk, Walter Stoeckmann, Diego Fontayne* PRODUCT PHOTOGRAPHER: *John Moldauer, Human Factors Industrial Design Inc.* MANUFACTURER: *Kash N Gold* MATERIALS: *Injection-Molded ABS, silicone* DESIGN YEAR: *1996* PRODUCTION YEAR: *1997* LAUNCH YEAR: *1997*

PAGE 40 PRODUCT: *Kenwood Multimedia Speakers* DESIGN FIRM: *ZIBA Design* DESIGNERS: *Sohrab Vossoughi, Iulius Lucaci* PRODUCT PHOTOGRAPHER: *Marcus Swanson* MANUFACTURER: *Kenwood USA* MATERIALS: *Injection-Molded ABS* DESIGN YEAR: *1995* PRODUCTION YEAR: *1996* LAUNCH YEAR: *1996*

PAGE 41 PRODUCT: *Simply Cinema ESC 300 Speakers* DESIGN FIRM: *Fitch Inc.* SENIOR DESIGNER/PROGRAM MANAGER: *David Gresham* DESIGNERS: *John Devanney, Sven Adolf* PRODUCT PHOTOGRAPHER: *John Shotwell* CLIENT/MANUFACTURER: *JBL*

PAGES 42, 43 PRODUCT: *Control Series Speakers* DESIGN FIRM: *Fitch Inc.* DESIGNERS: *Edwin Beck, Sven Adolph, John Devanney* PRODUCT PHOTOGRAPHER: *Thomas Wedell, Skolos/Wedell* CLIENT/MANUFACTURER: *JBL Consumer Products* DESIGN YEAR: *1996* PRODUCTION YEAR: *1996* LAUNCH YEAR: *1997*

PAGE 44 PRODUCT: *Multimedia Speaker System* DESIGN FIRM: *RKS Design Inc.* CLIENT/MANUFACTURER: *Harman Interactive Group/JBL* DESIGN YEAR: *1995* LAUNCH YEAR: *1995*

PAGE 45 PRODUCT: *Infinity Overture Series Home Theater Loudspeakers* DESIGN FIRM: *Ashcraft Design* ART DIRECTOR: *Daniel Ashcraft* DESIGNER: *Trung Phung* PRODUCT PHOTOGRAPHER: *David Slagle* CLIENT: *Infinity* MANUFACTURER: *Harman Manufacturing Group* DESIGN DATE: *8/95* PRODUCTION DATE: *4/96* LAUNCH DATE: *1/96*

PAGE 46 PRODUCT: *TapeStor External Tapedrive* DESIGN FIRM: *frogdesign, inc.* PRODUCT PHOTOGRAPHER: *frogdesign team* CLIENT: *Seagate Technology*

PAGE 47 DESIGN FIRM: *Lunar Design* DESIGNERS: *Tad Toulis, Andrew Zee, Mike Simmons, Scott Chamness of Lunar Design; Steve Dean, Demick Boyden, Steve Smithson of Silicon Graphics* PRODUCT PHOTOGRAPHER: *Rick English, English Photography* CLIENT/MANUFACTURER: *Silicon Graphics* DESIGN DATE: *1/96* PRODUCTION DATE: *10/96* LAUNCH DATE: *10/96*

PAGE 48 PRODUCT: *TV Set Top Box* DESIGN FIRM: *Design Edge* DESIGNER: *Philip Leverage* PRODUCT PHOTOGRAPHER: *Stence & Stence* CLIENT/MANUFACTURER: *Apple Computer Inc.* MATERIALS: *ABS acrylic plastic* DESIGN DATE: *6/95* PRODUCTION DATE: *12/95*

PAGE 49 DESIGN FIRM: *GVO, Inc.* DESIGNER: *Shawn Hanna* PRODUCT PHOTOGRAPHER: *Rick English* CLIENT: *Picture Tel* MANUFACTURER: *Solectron* MATERIALS: *Recyclable plastics* DESIGN YEAR: *1996* PRODUCTION YEAR: *1996* LAUNCH DATE: *10/96*

PAGE 50 PRODUCT: *ION Wearable Computer System (functional protoype)* DESIGN FIRM: *Engineering Design Research Center, Carnegie Mellon University* DESIGNERS: *Chris Kasabach, John Stivoric* PRODUCT PHOTOGRAPHER: *Jeff Macklin* CLIENT: *Advanced Research Projects Agency* MATERIALS: *Magnesium alloy rubber polycarbonate polypropylene* DESIGN DATE: *6/96* PRODUCTION DATE: *4/97*

PAGE 51 DESIGN FIRM: *Interform* DESIGNER: *Peter Muller* PRODUCT PHOTOGRAPHER: *Carter Dow* MANUFACTURER: *Astounding Technologies* MATERIALS: *Polycarbonate, ABS, santoprene* DESIGN YEAR: *1995* PRODUCTION YEAR: *1996* LAUNCH YEAR: *1997*

PAGE 52 PRODUCTS: *Network Server and Workstation* DESIGN FIRM: *Hauser, Inc.* ARTISTIC DIRECTOR: *Ron Pierce* DESIGNERS: *Edward Cruz, Barry Sween, Shaun Fynn* PRODUCT PHOTOGRAPHER: *Terry Sutherland, Sutherland Photo Design* CLIENT: *Panda Project* MATERIALS: *Structural foam, aluminum, ABS*

PAGE 53 PRODUCT: *External Hard Drive* DESIGN FIRM: *CI Design* ARTISTIC DIRECTOR: *Celine Keeble* DESIGNERS: *Jeff Wu, Hung Lee, Mich Chen* PRODUCT PHOTOGRAPHER: *Michael Jarrett, Michael Jarrett Studio* MANUFACTURER: *CI Design* MATERIALS: *Recyclable Sheet Metal, ABS Plastic* DESIGN DATE: *3/97* PRODUCTION DATE: *7/97* LAUNCH DATE: *8/97*

PAGE 54 DESIGN FIRM: *IDEO Product Development* ART DIRECTOR: *Scott Stropkay* DESIGNERS: *Scott Stropkay, David Weissburg, Michael Hess, Mark Nichols, David Privitera* PRODUCT PHOTOGRAPHER: *Tom Wedel* CLIENT/MANUFACTURER: *Polaroid Corporation* MATERIALS: *Cycoloy* DESIGN YEAR: *1996* LAUNCH DATE: *9/96*

PAGE 55 PRODUCT: *Cyclone Omnidirectional Scanner* DESIGN FIRM: *Altitude* ARTISTIC DIRECTOR: *Alan Ball* DESIGNERS: *Jonathan Marks, Drew Tosh, Phil Swift, Ian Jenkins* PRODUCT PHOTOGRAPHER: *Bill Albrecht* MANUFACTURER: *Symbol Technologies, Inc.* DESIGN DATE: *12/96*

PAGE 56 PRODUCT: *Sensu PDA Pen Device* DESIGN FIRM: *Design Edge* DESIGNER: *Mark Kimbrough* PRODUCT PHOTOGRAPHER: *Stence & Stence* MANUFACURER/CLIENT: *IDEC* MATERIALS: *Aluminum, Plexiglass* DESIGN DATE: *6/95* PRODUCTION DATE: *10/95*

PAGE 57 DESIGN FIRM: *Philips Design* LAUNCH DATE: *3/94*

PAGES 58, 59 PRODUCT: *Spanoto Moormann Tables* DESIGNER: *Jakob Gebert* MANUFACTURER: *Moormann Möbel–Produktions und–Handels GmbH* DESIGN YEAR: *1996* PRODUCTION YEAR: *1996* LAUNCH YEAR: *1996*

PAGE 60 PRODUCT: *Table de verre II* DESIGN FIRM: *Atelier d'Architecture Chaix Morel et Associatiés* DESIGNERS: *Philippe Chaix, Jean-Paul Morel* PRODUCT PHOTOGRAPHERS: *Philippe Chaix, Jean-Paul Morel* MANUFACTURER: *Forma* MATERIALS: *Glass, Steel* DESIGN YEAR: *1995* PRODUCTION YEAR: *1995* LAUNCH YEAR: *1995*

PAGE 61 PRODUCT: *Tempo Center Table* ARTISTIC DIRECTOR: *Samuel Coriat* DESIGNER: *Pascal Mourgue* CLIENT: *Artelano* MANUFACTURER: *Artelano* MATERIALS: *Beechwood, frosted glass* DESIGN YEAR: *1996* PRODUCTION YEAR: *1996* LAUNCH YEAR: *1996*

PAGE 62 PRODUCT: *Inflatable table* DESIGN FIRM: *Compana Objetos Ltda.* DESIGNERS: *Fernando Campana, Humberto Campana* PRODUCT PHOTOGRAPHER: *Andrés Otero* MANUFACTURER: *Campana Objetos Ltda.* MATERIALS: *PVC* DESIGN YEAR: *1996* PRODUCTION YEAR: *1996* LAUNCH YEAR: *1996*

PAGE 63 PRODUCT: *Slotted Café Table* DESIGN FIRM/MANUFACTURER: *Doghaus, Inc.* DESIGNERS: *Brian Hagiwara, Bret Baughman* PRODUCT PHOTOGRAPHER: *Brian Hagiwara* MATERIALS: *black-finished Finland plywood, Finland spruce* DESIGN DATE: *4/96* PRODUCTION DATE: *5/96* LAUNCH DATE: *9/96*

PAGES 64, 65 PRODUCT: *Less table* DESIGNER: *Jean Novel* PRODUCT PHOTOGRAPHER: *Studio Azzurro* MANUFACTURER: *Unifor, S.p.A.* MATERIALS: *Folded steel top with solid steel legs* DESIGN YEAR: *1994* PRODUCTION YEAR: *1994* LAUNCH YEAR: *1994*

PAGE 66 PRODUCT: *T.4.1. Armchair* ARTISTIC DIRECTOR: *Isabelle Millet* DESIGNER: *Olivier Leblois* PRODUCT PHOTOGRAPHER: *Quart de Poil'* CLIENT: *Quart de Poil'* MANUFACTURER: *Cayersberg Packaging* MATERIALS: *Corrugated cardboard* DESIGN YEAR: *1995* PRODUCTION YEAR: *1995* LAUNCH YEAR: *1995*

PAGE 67 PRODUCTS: *Table and seating* DESIGN FIRM: *Atelier Boris Bally* ARTISTIC DIRECTOR: *Boris Bally* DESIGNER: *Boris Bally* PRODUCT PHOTOGRAPHER: *David Smith* MANUFACTURER: *Versa-Fab Inc* MATERIALS: *Recycled Traffic Signs* DESIGN DATE: *4/96* PRODUCTION YEAR: *1996* LAUNCH YEAR: *1996*

PAGE 68 DESIGN FIRM: *Architecture + Furniture* ART DIRECTOR: *John Petrarca* DESIGNER: *Gregory Talmont* PRODUCT PHOTOGRAPHER: *Peter Mausa, Esto* CLIENT: *Kit & Gerry Laybourne* MATERIALS: *Sand Cast Aluminum Leather* DESIGN DATE: *2/94* PRODUCTION DATE: *4/94*

PAGE 69 DESIGN FIRM: *Art Center College of Design, Pasadena* INSTRUCTOR: *David Mocarski* DESIGNER: *Linda Mai* PRODUCT PHOTOGRAPHER: *Steven Heller, Art Center College of Design, Pasadena* MATERIALS: *Birch-veneer plywood, MDF, laminates* DESIGN YEAR: *1996* PRODUCTION YEAR: *1996*

PAGES 70, 71 DESIGN FIRMS: *Jhane Barnes, TZ Design, DMJ Rottet* DESIGNERS: *Jhane Barnes, Mark Goetz, Lauren Rottet* PRODUCT PHOTOGRAPHER: *Viewpoint Studios* MANUFACTURER: *Bernhardt* DESIGN DATE: *1/96* PRODUCTION DATE: *1/96* LAUNCH DATE: *6/96*

PAGE 72 PRODUCT: *Bubblewrap Chair* DESIGN FIRM: *Compana Objetos Ltda.* DESIGNERS: *Fernando Campana, Humberto Campana* PRODUCT PHOTOGRAPHER: *Andres Otero* MANUFACTURER: *Campana Objetos Ltda.* MATERIALS: *Electrostatic paint, chrome, steel, bubblewrap* DESIGN YEAR: *1995* PRODUCTION YEAR: *1995* LAUNCH YEAR: *1995*

PAGE 73 PRODUCT: *Knotted Chair* DESIGNER: *Marcel Wanders* PRODUCT PHOTOGRAPHER: *Robbie Kavanagh* MANUFACTURER: *Cappellini* MATERIALS: *Rope, carbon, aramide, epoxy*

PAGE 74 PRODUCTS: *A-1 Table, A-2 Chair* DESIGN FIRM: *Dale Frommelt Design* DESIGNER: *Dale Frommelt* PRODUCT PHOTOGRAPHER: *Kurtis Kracke* MATERIALS: *Plywood, metal screws*

PAGE 75 PRODUCTS: *Soattosopra and Zack coffee tables* DESIGNERS: *William K. Sawaya* MANUFACTURER: *Sawaya & Moroni S.p.A* MATERIALS: *cherrywood or mahogany veneer plywood, aluminum base* DESIGN YEAR: *1994* PRODUCTION YEAR: *1996* LAUNCH YEAR: *1996*

PAGE 76 PRODUCTS: *Magazine and Fly Two Sofas, MY Table* DESIGN FIRM: *MY-022 Ltd* DESIGNER: *Michael Young* PRODUCT PHOTOGRAPHER: *David Simmonds* MANUFACTURER: *MY-022* MATERIALS: *Metal, fabric, foam, wood* DESIGN YEAR: *1995 & 1996*

PAGE 77 (MIDDLE RIGHT) PRODUCT: *Table* DESIGN FIRM: *Kids' Studio* DESIGNER: *Allan Kazovsky* PRODUCT PHOTOGRAPHER: *Tom Bonner* MANUFACTURER: *Alfons Mousa* MATERIALS: *Finland birch plywood, Fin Color Plywood* DESIGN DATE: *3/94* PRODUCTION DATE: *9/94* LAUNCH DATE: *12/94*

PAGE 77 (TOP, MIDDLE LEFT, BOTTOM) DESIGN FIRM: *Kids' Studio* DESIGNER: *Alla Kazovsky* PRODUCT PHOTOGRAPHER: *Julie Taylor* CLIENTS: *Emily Blumental, Michael Gold* MANUFACTURER: *Acton Woodworks* MATERIALS: *Solid maple, maple-veneer plywood* DESIGN DATE: *3/96* PRODUCTION DATE: *12/96* LAUNCH DATE: *12/96*

PAGES 78, 79 DESIGN FIRM: *Daniel Taylor & Associates* DESIGNER: *Daniel Taylor* PRODUCT PHOTOGRAPHER: *Steve Perry, Rising Star* MANUFACTURER: *Contemporary American Furniture*

PAGE 80 DESIGN FIRM/MANUFACTURER: *BRO Designed Construction* ARTISTIC

DIRECTORS: *Joel Breaux* PRODUCT PHOTOGRAPHER: *BRO Designed Construction* CLIENT: *BJ Krivanek Art & Design* MATERIALS: *Aluminum, clear glass* DESIGN YEAR: *1996* PRODUCTION YEAR: *1995* LAUNCH DATE: *1/11/97*

PAGE 81 DESIGN FIRM: *Wagner Murray Architects* DESIGNER: *David Wagner* PRODUCT PHOTOGRAPHER: *Steve Knight* MANUFACTURER: *Piedmont Wood Products* MATERIALS: *Mahogany, reconstituted bernac* DESIGN YEAR: *1996* PRODUCTION YEAR: *1996* LAUNCH YEAR: *1996*

PAGE 82 DESIGN FIRM: *Art Center College of Design, Pasedena* INSTRUCTOR: *David Mocarski* DESIGNER: *Sami Hayek* PRODUCT PHOTOGRAPHER: *Steven Heller, Art Center College Of Design* MATERIALS: *Carbon Fiber and Aluminum* DESIGN DATE: *9/96*

PAGE 83 DESIGN FIRM: *Art Center College of Design, Pasadena* ART DIRECTOR: *David Mockarski* DESIGNER: *Arsenio Garcia-Monsalve* PRODUCT PHOTOGRAPHER: *Steven Heller, Art Center College of Design, Pasadena* MATERIALS: *Birch-veneer plywood, stainless steel* DESIGN DATE: *3/96* PRODUCTION DATE: *4/96* LAUNCH DATE: *4/96*

PAGE 84 (TOP LEFT) DESIGN FIRM: *Art Center College of Design, Pasadena* ART DIRECTOR: *David Mockarski* DESIGNER: *Michelle Chong* PRODUCT PHOTOGRAPHER: *Steven Heller, Art Center College of Design, Pasadena* MATERIALS: *Purple heart wood, aluminum* DESIGN YEAR: *1996* PRODUCTION YEAR: *1996*

PAGE 84 (TOP RIGHT) DESIGN FIRM: *Art Center College of Design, Pasadena* ART DIRECTORS: *David Mocarski* DESIGNER: *Julien Egger* PRODUCT PHOTOGRAPHER: *Steven Heller, Art Center College of Design, Pasadena* MATERIALS: *MDF, plywood, veneer, aluminum* DESIGN DATE: *7/96* PRODUCTION DATE: *8/96*

PAGE 84 (BOTTOM) DESIGN FIRM: *BDI* DESIGNER: *Al Glass* PRODUCT PHOTOGRAPHER: *Michael Latil* MANUFACTURER: *Bdi* MATERIALS: *Glass & Steel* LAUNCH DATE: *9/96, 2/97*

PAGE 85 PRODUCTS: *Lob Seat, Kisos Chair, Zig Armchair* DESIGNER: *Efi Benbassa* PRODUCT PHOTOGRAPHER: *Hastudio Hajerushlmi, Hastudio Hajerushlmi, Ltd.* MANUFACTURER: *Efi Benbassa Design Studio* MATERIALS: *Steel, polyurethane foam, fabric* DESIGN YEAR: *1995/6* PRODUCTION YEAR: *1996/7* LAUNCH YEAR: *1996/7*

PAGES 86, 87 PRODUCTS: *Dr. No Chair, Dr. Na Table, Miss Trap Table, Miss Trap Chair* ART DIRECTOR: *Philippe Starck* MANUFACTURER: *Kartell* MATERIALS: *Wood, polypropylene* DESIGN YEAR: *1995* PRODUCTION YEAR: *1996* LAUNCH YEAR: *1997*

PAGE 88 PRODUCTS: *Chairs, Stool, Chaise Lounge* DESIGN FIRM/MANUFACTURER: *Yellow Diva* DESIGNERS: *James Davis, David Walley* MATERIALS: *Wool, dacron wadding, foam, wooden frames, plywood, metal weight*

PAGE 89 DESIGNER: *Maurizio Favetta* PRODUCT PHOTOGRAPHER: *Fotorama* MANUFACTURER: *King Size by Lisar* MATERIALS: *Cast aluminum, plexiglass, acrylic, leather* DESIGN YEAR: *1992* PRODUCTION YEAR: *1993* LAUNCH YEAR: *1993*

PAGE 90 PRODUCT: *Sea Table system* DESIGNER: *Carlo Bartoli* PRODUCT PHOTOGRAPHER: *Miro Zagnoli* MANUFACTURER: *Segis S.p.A./Lowenstein* MATERIALS: *Aluminum, laquered tops, polypropylene feet* DESIGN YEAR: *1995* PRODUCTION YEAR: *1996* LAUNCH YEAR: *1996*

PAGE 91 PRODUCTS: *Longframe Chaise Lounge, Armframe Chair* DESIGNER: *Alberto Meda* PRODUCT PHOTOGRAPHER: *Miro Zagnoli, Studio Controluce* MANUFACTURER: *Alias*

PAGES 92, 93 PRODUCT: *Aeron Office Chair* DESIGNERS: *Don Chadwick, Bill Stumpf* PRODUCT PHOTOGRAPHERS: *Nick Merrick, Hedrich Blessing* MANUFACTURER: *Herman Miller, Inc.* DESIGN YEAR: *1994* PRODUCTION DATE: *10/94* LAUNCH DATE: *10/94*

PAGES 94, 95 DESIGN FIRM: *Parkersulic* DESIGNER: *François Sulic* PRODUCT PHOTOGRAPHER: *Michael Christmas* MANUFACTURER: *Simm/Brendan* MATERIALS:

Maple, steel DESIGN DATE: *3/94* PRODUCTION DATE: *8/94*

PAGE 96 PRODUCT: *Conference Table* DESIGN FIRM: *Alternativ Studio* DESIGNER: *Péter Vajda* PRODUCT PHOTOGRAPHER: *Dániel Horváth*

PAGE 97 PRODUCT: *Butterfly Table* DESIGN FIRM: *Osburn Design* DESIGNER: *Steven Osburn* PRODUCT PHOTOGRAPHER: *Terrence McCarthy, SUNSET MAGAZINE Photo Dept.* MANUFACTURER: *Nico Interiors* MATERIALS: *Gold and rose-dyed Finland birch veneer, ebony-stained solid maple* DESIGN YEAR: *1993* PRODUCTION YEAR: *1994* LAUNCH YEAR: *1996*

PAGE 98 (TOP) PRODUCT: *OXO PC Computer Cart* DESIGNER: *Antonio Citterio* MANUFACTURER: *Kartell* MATERIALS: *Aluminum, steel, polypropylene* DESIGN YEAR: *1997* PRODUCTION YEAR: *1997* LAUNCH YEAR: *1997*

PAGE 98 (BOTTOM) PRODUCT: *Sistema Mauna Kea* DESIGNER: *Vico Magistrelli* MANUFACTURER: *Kartell* MATERIALS: *Aluminum, steel, polypropylene* DESIGN YEAR: *1997* PRODUCTION YEAR: *1997* LAUNCH YEAR: *1997*

PAGE 99 DESIGN FIRM: *KI* PRODUCT PHOTOGRAPHER: *KI* CLIENT: *KI* MANUFACTURER: *KI* MATERIALS: *Steel-enamel Nylin particle board* DESIGN DATE: *3/95* PRODUCTION DATE: *9/95* LAUNCH DATE: *6/95*

PAGES 100, 101 PRODUCT: *Wave chairs* DESIGN FIRM: *The Burdick Group* DESIGNERS: *Bruce Burdick, Susan Burdick, Johnson Chow* CLIENT: *Itoki Co. Ltd*

PAGE 102 DESIGN FIRM: *Sigmag* DESIGNER: *Luke Raymond* CLIENT: *Sigmag* MANUFACTURER: *Luke Raymond* MATERIALS: *Wood, metal, glass* DESIGN DATE: *9/97* PRODUCTION DATE: *12/97* LAUNCH DATE: *1/97*

PAGE 103 DESIGN FIRM: *Studio eg* DESIGNER: *Erez Steinberg* PRODUCT PHOTOGRAPHER: *Sharon Risdorf Photography* MANUFACTURER: *Studio eg* DESIGN DATE: *10/95* PRODUCTION DATE: *1/96* LAUNCH DATE: *1/96*

PAGES 104, 105 DESIGNER: *Manfred Herrmann* MANUFACTURER: *Dauphin* MATERIALS: *Aluminum, steel, polyurethane foam, plywood* DESIGN DATE: *3/95* PRODUCTION DATE: *3/97* LAUNCH DATE: *10/95*

PAGES 106, 107 PRODUCT: *Café chair* DESIGN FIRM: *The Burdick Group* DESIGNERS: *Bruce Burdick, Susan Burdick, Johnson Chow* MANUFACTURER: *Itoki Co. Ltd.* MATERIALS: *Plastics, aluminum*

PAGE 107 DESIGN FIRM: *The Burdick Group* DESIGNERS: *Susan Burdick, Bruce Burdick* PRODUCT PHOTOGRAPHER: *Studio Convex* MANUFACTURER: *Itoki Co Ltd* MATERIALS: *Aluminum, urethane foam*

PAGES 108, 109 PRODUCT: *Stacking Chair* DESIGN FIRM: *Thomas J. Newhouse Design* DESIGNER: *Tom Newhouse* PRODUCT PHOTOGRAPHERS: *Nick Merrick, Hedrich Blessing* CLIENT: *Herman Miller SQA* MANUFACTURER: *Herman Miller SQA* MATERIALS: *Polypropylene, steel* DESIGN DATE: *10/95* PRODUCTION DATE: *6/96* LAUNCH DATE: *6/96*

PAGES 110 (TOP, BOTTOM), 111 (TOP) DESIGN FIRM: *Art Center College of Design, Pasadena* ART DIRECTOR: *David Mocarski* DESIGNER: *Dario Antonioni* PRODUCT PHOTOGRAPHER: *Steven Heller, Art Center College of Design, Pasadena* MATERIALS: *Steel, maple, mahogany, aluminum, glass* DESIGN DATE: *9/96*

PAGE 110 (MIDDLE LEFT, MIDDLE RIGHT) DESIGN FIRM: *Art Center College of Design, Pasadena* ART DIRECTOR: *David Mocarski* DESIGNER: *Julien Egger* PRODUCT PHOTOGRAPHER: *Steven Heller, Art Center College of Design, Pasadena* MATERIALS: *MDF, plywood, veneer, aluminum* DESIGN DATE: *7/96* PRODUCTION DATE: *8/96*

PAGE 112 PRODUCT: *Desk* DESIGN FIRM: *J3 Design* DESIGNER: *John Jaqua* MATERIALS: *MDF, aluminum, non-toxic sealant, plastics, cotton fabric*

PAGE 113 DESIGN FIRM: *KI* PRODUCT PHOTOGRAPHER: *KI* CLIENT: *KI* MANUFACTURER: *KI* MATERIALS: *Steel frame, die-cast aluminum, urethane foam* DESIGN DATE: *12/96* PRODUCTION DATE: *12/97* LAUNCH DATE: *6/97*

PAGE 114 DESIGN FIRM: *Microsoft Hardware Design Group* PRODUCT

PHOTOGRAPHER: *Michael Jones* MANUFACTURER: *Microsoft* MATERIALS: *ABS plastic* DESIGN DATE: *10/95* PRODUCTION DATE: *5/97* LAUNCH DATE: *10/97*

PAGE 115 DESIGN FIRM: *Wagner Murray Architects* DESIGNER: *David Wagner* MANUFACTURER: *Prototype Backgammon Board* MATERIALS: *20/24 clear anodized aluminum, T4 grade brass* DESIGN YEAR: *1995* PRODUCTION YEAR: *1995*

PAGE 116 DESIGN FIRM: *Glass & Glass Inc./Gardner Keaton Incorporated* DESIGNERS: *Al Glass, Jim Keaton* MANUFACTURER: *Glass & Glass Inc.* MATERIALS: *Glass, stainless steel, nickel plated brass* DESIGN DATE: *9/96* PRODUCTION DATE: *1/97* LAUNCH DATE: *2/97*

PAGE 117 (TOP) DESIGN FIRM: *Smart Design, Inc.* DESIGNERS: *Scott Henderson, David Farrage, Davin Stowell* MANUFACTURER: *Alps Electric USA Inc.* MATERIALS: *Injection-molded ABS, injection-molded santoprene* DESIGN DATE: *2/96* PRODUCTION DATE: *10/96* LAUNCH DATE: *11/97*

PAGE 117 (BOTTOM) DESIGN FIRM: *Karo Design Resources, Inc.* DESIGNERS: *Greg Corrigan, Robert Jarshke* PRODUCT PHOTOGRAPHER: *John Sinal* MANUFACTURER: *Advanced Gravis Computer Technology Ltd.* MATERIALS: *Injection-molded plastics* DESIGN DATE: *4/94* PRODUCTION DATE: *8/94* LAUNCH DATE: *8/94*

PAGE 118 PRODUCT: *Modular Toy* DESIGN FIRM: *Vanderbyl Design* DESIGNER: *Michael Vanderbyl* MANUFACTURER: *George Beylerian Productions* MATERIALS: *Wood, metal*

PAGE 119 PRODUCT: *Illuminated Doorbell Buttons* DESIGN FIRM: *Spore* DESIGNERS: *Tom Gordon, Theodore Pierson* PRODUCT PHOTOGRAPHER: *Jim Linna, Linna Photographics* MANUFACTURER: *Spore* MATERIALS: *Elastometric plastic, aluminum* DESIGN YEAR: *1994* PRODUCTION DATE: *10/96* LAUNCH DATE: *1/97*

PAGE 120 DESIGN FIRM: *Inflate* DESIGNER: *Nick Crosbie* PRODUCT PHOTOGRAPHER: *Jason Tozer* MANUFACTURER: *Inflate* DESIGN DATE: *10/95* PRODUCTION DATE: *11/95* LAUNCH DATE: *11/95*

PAGE 121 DESIGN FIRM: *555 Design* DESIGNER: *James Geier, principal* CLIENT: *Automatic Inc.* MANUFACTURER: *555 Manufacturing* MATERIALS: *Laminated glass, stainless steel* DESIGN DATE: *4/96* PRODUCTION DATE: *5/96* LAUNCH DATE: *5/96*

PAGE 122 PRODUCT: *Carafe* DESIGN FIRM: *Ancona Z Inc.* DESIGNERS: *Bruce Ancona, Joseph Gasparino, Jane Ancona* PRODUCT PHOTOGRAPHER: *Peter Hogg* CLIENT: *B. Via International* MATERIAL: *Frosted Polypropylene, thermal liner* DESIGN DATE: *12/94* PRODUCTION DATE: *1/97* LAUNCH DATE: *1/97*

PAGE 123 PRODUCT: *Good Grips Tea Kettle* DESIGN FIRM: *Smart Design, Inc.* DESIGNERS: *Vanessa Sica, Mari Ando, Davin Stowell, C. Scott Bolden* PRODUCT PHOTOGRAPHER: *Peter Medliek* MANUFACTURER: *OXO International* MATERIALS: *Stainless steel phenolic handle, santoprene overmold nylon cover, silicone gaskets* DESIGN YEAR: *1996* PRODUCTION YEAR: *1996* LAUNCH YEAR: *1996*

PAGE 124 DESIGN FIRM: *Ecco Design, Inc.* DESIGNERS: *Eric Chan, Jeff Miller* PRODUCT PHOTOGRAPHER: *Corning* CLIENT: *Revereware, Corning Consumer Products Division* MATERIALS: *Stainless steel, copper, phenolic plastic* DESIGN YEAR: *1995* PRODUCTION YEAR: *1996* LAUNCH YEAR: *1996*

PAGE 125 (LEFT) PRODUCT: *Tea Kettle* DESIGN FIRM: *Porcelli Associates Inc.* ART DIRECTOR: *V. Porcelli* PRODUCT PHOTOGRAPHER: *Laurie Rubin* MANUFACTURER: *Dansk International Designs Ltd.* MATERIALS: *Silver-plated brass* DESIGN YEAR: *1987* PRODUCTION YEAR: *1988* LAUNCH YEAR: *1988*

PAGE 125 (RIGHT) PRODUCT: *Tea Set and Tea Kettle* DESIGN FIRM: *Porcelli Associates Inc.* ART DIRECTORS: *V. Porcelli* MANUFACTURER: *Dansk International Designs Ltd.* MATERIALS: *Stainless-steel body phenolic handle* DESIGN YEAR: *1980* PRODUCTION YEAR: *1986* LAUNCH YEAR: *1986*

PAGE 126 PRODUCT: *Carafe* DESIGN FIRM: *Graves Design* DESIGNER: *Michael Graves* PRODUCT PHOTOGRAPHER: *Carlo Paggiarino, Saccardo Carlo & Figli* CLIENT: *Alessi S.p.A.* MANUFACTURER: *Alessi S.p.A.* MATERIALS: *ABS plastic* DESIGN DATE: *1/94* PRODUCTION DATE: *5/95* LAUNCH DATE: *10/95*

PAGE 127 PRODUCTS: *Tea Kettle and Coffee Pot* DESIGN FIRM: *Graves Design* DESIGNER: *Michael Graves* PRODUCT PHOTOGRAPHER: *Carlo Paggiarino, Saccardo Carlo & Figli* MANUFACTURER: *Alessi S.p.A.* MATERIALS: *Aluminum, polyamide* DESIGN YEAR: *1995* PRODUCTION DATE: *11/96* LAUNCH DATE: *12/96*

PAGE 128 PRODUCTS: *Citrus Press, Coffee Maker, Kettle, Toaster, Sunrise Toaster* DESIGN FIRM: *Philips Design Department* MANUFACTURER: *Philips-Alessi* MATERIALS: *Recyclable PC (plastic), water soluable, cadmium-free inks, metal* LAUNCH DATE: *9/96*

PAGE 129 PRODUCT: *Lush Lilly trays* DESIGN FIRM: *Lunar Design* DESIGNERS: *Yves Behar, Jeff Hoefer, Darren Blum, David Malina* PRODUCT PHOTOGRAPHER: *Rick English* MATERIALS: *Recycled polypropylene* DESIGN YEAR: *1996*

PAGE 130 PRODUCT: *Dinnerware* DESIGN FIRM: *Calvin Klein* MANUFACTURER: *Calvin Klein Home* MATERIALS: *ceramic, glass, stainless steel* LAUNCH YEAR: *1997*

PAGE 131 PRODUCT: *Waste Bin* DESIGN FIRM: *Beyond Design Inc.* DESIGNER: *Michael Prince* PRODUCT PHOTOGRAPHER: *Dan Warkenthien, Warkenthien Photography* MANUFACTURER: *Beyond Design 2* MATERIALS: *Polypropylene with 20% recycled regrind* DESIGN DATE: *12/15/95* PRODUCTION DATE: *8/01/96* LAUNCH DATE: *8/01/96*

PAGE 132 PRODUCTS: *Vertigo Vase and Flutso Square Bowl* DESIGN FIRM: *Vanderbyl Design* DESIGNER: *Michael Vanderbyl* PRODUCT PHOTOGRAPHER: *Karl Petzke* CLIENT: *Pentimento* MANUFACTURER: *Earth Needs Ltd* MATERIALS: *White clay, matte glazes* DESIGN YEAR: *1996* PRODUCTION YEAR: *1997* LAUNCH YEAR: *1997*

PAGE 133 PRODUCT: *Faitoo Wall-Mounted Kitchen Utensil System* DESIGNER: *Philippe Starck* PRODUCT PHOTOGRAPHER: *Santi Caleca* MANUFACTURER: *Alessi S.p.A.* MATERIALS: *Ceramics, stainless steel* DESIGN YEAR: *1994* PRODUCTION YEAR: *1996* LAUNCH YEAR: *1996*

PAGES 134, 135 PRODUCT: *Coolspot Trivets* DESIGN FIRM: *Tupperware* DESIGNER: *Douglas Laib* MANUFACTURER: *Tupperware* MATERIALS: *Melamine* DESIGN YEAR: *1993* PRODUCTION YEAR: *1994* LAUNCH YEAR: *1994*

PAGE 136 PRODUCT: *BBQ Utensils* DESIGN FIRM/MANUFACTURER: *Zelco Industries Inc.* DESIGNERS: *Noel Zeller, Nicole Zeller* MATERIALS: *18/8 stainless steel, plastic*

PAGE 137 (TOP) PRODUCT: *Micromug Coffee Mug* DESIGN FIRM: *Tupperware* DESIGNER: *Douglas Laib* MANUFACTURER: *Tupperware* DESIGN YEAR: *1994* PRODUCTION YEAR: *1994* LAUNCH YEAR: *1994*

PAGE 137 (BOTTOM) PRODUCT: *Serving Fork and Spoon* DESIGN FIRM/MANUFACTURER: *MacBain Art Metal* ART DIRECTOR: *Kenneth MacBain* PRODUCT PHOTOGRAPHER: *Kenneth MacBain* MATERIALS: *Sterling silver, epoxy resin* DESIGN YEAR: *1997* PRODUCTION YEAR: *1997* LAUNCH YEAR: *1997*

PAGE 138 PRODUCT: *Thule Vase* DESIGNER: *Olivier Gagnère* PRODUCT PHOTOGRAPHER: *Dominique Cohas* MANUFACTURER: *Porcelaines Bernardaud* MATERIAL: *Bisque (matte porcelain)* DESIGN YEAR: *1994* PRODUCTION YEAR: *1994* LAUNCH YEAR: *1994*

PAGE 139 PRODUCT: *Western Perforated Series* DESIGN FIRM/MANUFACTURER: *555 Design* DESIGNER: *James Geier* MATERIALS: *Steel* DESIGN DATE: *3/94* PRODUCTION DATE: *4/94* LAUNCH DATE: *4/94*

PAGES 140, 141 PRODUCTS: *Trays, Plates, Bowls, Coasters* DESIGNER: *Karim Rashid* CLIENT: *Nambe Mills* MATERIALS: *Mixed-metal alloy (no silver, lead or pewter)* DESIGN YEAR: *1995* PRODUCTION YEAR: *1996*

PAGES 142, 143 DESIGNER: *Boris Bally* PRODUCT PHOTOGRAPHER: *David Smith* CLIENT: *Atelier Boris Bally* MANUFACTURER: *Atelier Boris Bally* MATERIALS: *Recycled aluminum traffic signs* DESIGN YEAR: *1995* PRODUCTION YEAR: *1996* LAUNCH YEAR: *1996*

PAGES 144, 145 PRODUCT: *Household Squeegee, Brushes, Dust Pan* DESIGN FIRM:

Smart Design, Inc. DESIGNERS: *Scott Henderson, David Farrage, David Stowell* PRODUCT PHOTOGRAPHER: *Peter Medliek* MANUFACTURER: *OXO International* MATERIALS: *Injection-molded polypropylene, injection-molded santoprene* DESIGN DATE: *2/95* PRODUCTION DATE: *11/95* LAUNCH DATE: *1/96*

PAGE 146 PRODUCT: *Cacti Orange Juicer* DESIGN FIRM: *Gear Atelier* ARTISTIC DIRECTOR: *May Wong* DESIGNERS: *May Wong, Dennis Chan* PRODUCT PHOTOGRAPHER: *Peter Lau* MATERIALS: *Polypropylene* DESIGN DATE: *4/95* PRODUCTION DATE: *7/95* LAUNCH YEAR: *8/95*

PAGE 147 PRODUCT: *Letter opener* DESIGN FIRM/MANUFACTURER: *Vilmain + Klinger* ART DIRECTOR: *Judy Vilmain* DESIGNERS: *David Klinger, Judy Vilmain* PRODUCT PHOTOGRAPHER: *Rick Sippel* MATERIALS: *Aluminum*

PAGES 148, 149 PRODUCT: *Food Storage Jars* DESIGNER: *Robert Mayercheck* PRODUCT PHOTOGRAPHER: *Rich Lasalle, Lasalle Studio* MANUFACTURER: *Flotool Corporation* MATERIALS: *Polypropylene, PET* DESIGN YEAR: *1993* PRODUCTION DATE: *1/94* LAUNCH DATE: *1/94*

PAGE 150 PRODUCT: *Wet n' Dry Carrier* DESIGN FIRM/MANUFACTURER: *Tupperware* DESIGNER: *Anita Liu* PRODUCT PHOTOGRAPHER: *Douglas M. Laib* DESIGN YEAR: *1995* PRODUCTION YEAR: *1996* LAUNCH YEAR: *1996*

PAGE 151 (TOP) PRODUCT: *YP Lunch Pack* DESIGN FIRM: *ZIBA Design* DESIGNERS: *Sohrab Vossoughi, Henry Chin, Jan Hippen* PRODUCT PHOTOGRAPHER: *Michael Jones* MANUFACTURER: *Youth Plastic Works* MATERIALS: *Injection-molded ABS plastic* DESIGN YEAR: *1994* PRODUCTION YEAR: *1994* LAUNCH YEAR: *1994*

PAGE 151 (BOTTOM) PRODUCT: *Storage Locker* DESIGN FIRM: *Product Insight, Inc.* DESIGNERS: *Bryan Hotaling, Jon Rossman* PRODUCT PHOTOGRAPHER: *Gary Arruda* CLIENT: *Tucker Housewares* MANUFACTURER: *Tucker Housewares* MATERIALS: *Polypropylene ABS* DESIGN DATE: *1/94* PRODUCTION DATE: *9/94* LAUNCH DATE: *9/94*

PAGE 152 (TOP LEFT, BOTTOM LEFT, BOTTOM RIGHT) PRODUCT: *Cook Surface and Oven* DESIGN FIRM: *Design Central* ART DIRECTOR: *Don Falk* DESIGNERS: *Gregg Davis, Pete Koloski, Thornton Lothrop, Steve Paletti of Design Central; Ron Zimmerman of Information Design Group* PRODUCT PHOTOGRAPHER: *Larry Friar, Friar & Associates* CLIENT: *GE Appliances Europe* MANUFACTURER: *GE Appliances Europe* MATERIALS: *Stainless steel, glass, rubber* DESIGN YEAR: *1996* PRODUCTION YEAR: *1996* LAUNCH DATE: *2/96*

PAGE 152 (TOP RIGHT) PRODUCT: *Ovens* DESIGN FIRM: *Roudebush Design Associates* DESIGNER: *Richard Roudebush* PRODUCT PHOTOGRAPHER: *Sparks Houser* MANUFACTURER: *Jenn-Air Corporation* DESIGN DATE: *3/95* LAUNCH DATE: *3/96*

PAGE 153 PRODUCT: *Toplifter Can Opener and Corkscrew* DESIGN FIRM: *Tupperware* DESIGNER: *Douglas M. Laib* MANUFACTURER: *Tupperware* DESIGN YEAR: *1993* PRODUCTION YEAR: *1994* LAUNCH YEAR: *1994*

PAGE 154 PRODUCT: *Toast Logic Toaster* DESIGN FIRM: *frogdesign, inc.* MANUFACTURER: *Sunbeam/Oster* MATERIALS: *Talc-filled polypropylene, glass-filled thermoset polyester, BMC, Schott Borosilicate glass with IR reflective coating, tin-plated steel, corrugated nickel-chrome ribbon on mica cards* LAUNCH YEAR: *1996*

PAGE 155 PRODUCT: *Smart Power Hand Mixer* DESIGN FIRM: *Smart Design, Inc.* DESIGNERS: *Scott Henderson, Tucker Viemeister* PRODUCT PHOTOGRAPHER: *Peter Medliek* MANUFACTURER: *Cuisinart Corporation* MATERIALS: *Injection-molded polypropylene, injection-molded ABS* DESIGN DATE: *2/94* PRODUCTION DATE: *11/94* LAUNCH DATE: *1/95*

PAGE 156 (TOP LEFT, TOP RIGHT) PRODUCT: *Iron* DESIGN FIRM: *IDEO Product Development* DESIGNER: *Richard Howarth* PRODUCT PHOTOGRAPHER: *Rick English, Rick English Pictures* CLIENT: *Matsushita* MATERIALS: *Injection-molded 75% zinc/25% polypropylene blend for main body, santoprene grip, die-cast aluminum baseplate* DESIGN DATE: *10/95*

PAGE 156 (BOTTOM LEFT) PRODUCT: *Sure Grip Fire Extinguisher* DESIGN FIRM: *Product Genesis, Inc.* DESIGNERS: *Clay Burns, Victor Cheung, Paul*

Sabin, Susannah Gardner, Cliff Lansil, Ken Feene PRODUCT PHOTOGRAPHER: *Peter Rice* MANUFACTURER: *First Alert* MATERIALS: *Nylon, steel,core, nitrile* DESIGN YEAR: *1996* PRODUCTION YEAR: *1996* LAUNCH YEAR: *1996*

PAGE 156 PRODUCT: *Water Purifier* DESIGN FIRM: *Product Genesis, Inc.* DESIGNERS: *Diane Branczaio, Susannah Gardner, Matthew Hern of Product Genesis; Frank Lubrano, David Sykes, Charles Heing, Dave Snow of Fountainhead Technologies* MANUFACTURER: *Fountainhead Technologies, Inc.* MATERIALS: *Plastic* DESIGN YEAR: *1994* PRODUCTION YEAR: *1994* LAUNCH DATE: *12/94*

PAGE 157 PRODUCT: *Iron* DESIGN FIRM: *IDEO Product Development* DESIGNER: *Richard Howarth* PRODUCT PHOTOGRAPHER: *Rick English, Rick English Pictures* CLIENT: *Matsushita* MATERIALS: *Injection-molded 75% zinc/25% polypropylene blend for main body, santoprene grip, die-cast aluminum baseplate* DESIGN DATE: *10/95*

PAGES 158, 159 PRODUCTS: *Textiles* DESIGN FIRM: *Lori Weitzner Design* DESIGNER: *Lori Weitzner* MANUFACTURER: *Larsen Inc.* MATERIALS: *Textile Collection*

PAGES 160, 161 DESIGN FIRM: *Harkavy & Associates* DESIGNER: *Christine Vanderhurd* PRODUCT PHOTOGRAPHER: *Scott Chaney* MANUFACTURER: *Christine Vanderhurd* MATERIALS: *100% hand-tufted sculpted wool* DESIGN YEAR: *1996* PRODUCTION YEAR: *1996* LAUNCH YEAR: *1996*

PAGES 160, 161 PRODUCT: *Rugs* DESIGNER: *Vicki Simon* PRODUCT PHOTOGRAPHER: *Cesar Rubio* MATERIALS: *100% Wool* DESIGN DATE: *1/94* PRODUCTION DATE: *1/94* LAUNCH DATE: *4/1/94*

PAGE 162 PRODUCT: *Mechanic's Creeper* DESIGN FIRM: *Michael W. Young Associates, Inc.* DESIGNERS: *Wei Young, Chig Ping Hsia, Sheng Fu Lee* CLIENT: *Detailed Designs* MANUFACTURER: *Detailed Designs* MATERIALS: *ABS, glass filaments* DESIGN YEAR: *1994* PRODUCTION YEAR: *1995* LAUNCH YEAR: *1995*

PAGE 163 PRODUCT: *Screw Driver and Bits* DESIGN FIRM: *Karo Design Resources, Inc.* DESIGNERS: *Greg Corrigan, Karen Winfield, Barry Marshall* PRODUCT PHOTOGRAPHER: *Tony Hurley* MANUFACTURER: *Winsire Enterprises Corporation* MATERIALS: *Injection-molded triax, ABS/nylon blend* DESIGN DATE: *1/96* PRODUCTION DATE: *4/96* LAUNCH DATE: *4/96*

PAGE 164 (TOP) PRODUCT: *D-Series Pistol* DESIGN FIRM: *Group Four Design* DESIGNERS: *Paul Metaxatos, Robert Bruno* PRODUCT PHOTOGRAPHER: *Rick Whittey Photography* CLIENT: *Ingersoll-Rand* MATERIALS: *30% glass filled nylon* DESIGN YEAR: *1996* PRODUCTION YEAR: *1997* LAUNCH YEAR: *1997*

PAGE 164 (MIDDLE) PRODUCT: *Plyers* DESIGN FIRM: *Interform* DESIGNER: *Peter Muller* PRODUCT PHOTOGRAPHER: *Cary Croopnick, Interform* CLIENT: *Simple Solutions* MANUFACTURER: *Plastics Korea* MATERIALS: *ABS* DESIGN YEAR: *1995* PRODUCTION YEAR: *1996* LAUNCH YEAR: *1996*

PAGE 164 (BOTTOM) PRODUCT: *Pliers* DESIGN FIRM: *Bally Design Inc.* DESIGNER: *Alex Bally* PRODUCT PHOTOGRAPHER: *Dave Smith* MANUFACTURER: *Applied Concepts* DESIGN YEAR: *1993* PRODUCTION YEAR: *1994* LAUNCH YEAR: *1994*

PAGE 165 PRODUCT: *Food Cart* DESIGN FIRM: *Acme City Carts* DESIGNERS: *Bruce Yelaska, Dan Friedlander* MATERIAL: *Stainless steel, recycled plastics* DESIGN YEAR: *1994* PRODUCTION YEAR: *1994* LAUNCH YEAR: *1994*

PAGE 166 PRODUCT: *Industrial Computer* DESIGN FIRM: *Lunar Design* PRODUCT PHOTOGRAPHER: *Rick English* MANUFACTURER: *Acuson Corporation*

PAGE 167 PRODUCT: *Datavisor 80* DESIGN FIRM: *ION Design* DESIGNERS: *Mario Tucrhi, Scott Salmon, Anthony Dibitonoto, Steven Bellofatto* PRODUCT PHOTOGRAPHER: *Jeffrey Goldman* MANUFACTURER: *n-Vision* MATERIALS: *Cast urethane, machined aluminum, nylon, EVA elastomer* DESIGN DATE: *9/96* PRODUCTION DATE: *10/96* LAUNCH DATE: *12/96*

PAGE 168 PRODUCT: *Megalux Lighting System* DESIGN FIRM: *Ottenwälder und Ottenwälder* DESIGNER: *Ottenwälder und Ottenwälder* PRODUCT PHOTOGRAPHER:

Harold Reich, Reich & Partner CLIENT: *AEG Lichttechnik GmbH* MATERIALS: *Aluminum* DESIGN YEAR: *1994* PRODUCTION YEAR: *1994* LAUNCH YEAR: *1994*
PAGE 169 PRODUCT: *X97 Hanging Lamp* DESIGN FIRM/MANUFACTURER: *modulor s.a.* ART DIRECTOR/DESIGNER: *Gaspar Glusberg* PRODUCT PHOTOGRAPHER: *Gaspar Glusberg* MATERIALS: *Iron sheeting, siliconed rubber, aluminum* DESIGN YEAR: *1988*

PAGE 170 PRODUCT: *Floor Lamp* DESIGN FIRM/MANUFACTURER: *Aqua Creations* ART DIRECTOR: *Albi Serfaty* DESIGNER: *Ayala S. Serfaty* PRODUCT PHOTOGRAPHER: *Albi Serfaty* MATERIALS: *Silk, steel*

PAGE 171 (TOP) PRODUCT: *UFO hanging lamp* DESIGN FIRM/MANUFACTURER: *Inflate* DESIGNER: *Nick Crosbie* PRODUCT PHOTOGRAPHER: *Jason Tozer* MATERIALS: *PVC film, polypropylene* DESIGN YEAR: *1996* PRODUCTION YEAR: *1996* LAUNCH YEAR: *1996*

PAGE 171 (BOTTOM) PRODUCT: *Lily Floor lamp* DESIGN FIRM/MANUFACTURER: *Inflate* DESIGNER: *Michael Sodeau* PRODUCT PHOTOGRAPHER: *Jason Tozer* MATERIALS: *PVC film*

PAGE 172 PRODUCT: *Yellow Gel Lantern Lamp* DESIGN FIRM: *Doghaus, Inc.* DESIGNERS: *Brian Hagiwara, Bret Baughman* PRODUCT PHOTOGRAPHER: *Brian Hagiwara* MANUFACTURER: *Doghaus, Inc.* MATERIALS: *Black powder-coated wire, lighting gels* DESIGN YEAR: *1996* PRODUCTION YEAR: *1997* LAUNCH YEAR: *1997*

PAGE 173 PRODUCTS: *Lighting Fixtures* DESIGN FIRM: *Pesce Ltd* DESIGNER: *Gaetano Pesce* PRODUCT PHOTOGRAPHER: *Veretta Cobbler* MANUFACTURER: *Pesce Ltd/Fish Design* MATERIALS: *Polyurethane Resin* DESIGN YEAR: *1996* PRODUCTION YEAR: *1996* LAUNCH YEAR: *1997*

PAGE 174 PRODUCT DESIGN: *Lightcolumn Range of Outdoor Lighting* DESIGN FIRM: *Philips Design Department* MANUFACTURER: *Philips* LAUNCH DATE: *9/95*

PAGE 175 PRODUCT: *Resaurant Lighting* DESIGN FIRM: *Krohn Design* PROJECT ARCHITECTS: *ROTO Architects* DESIGNER: *Lisa Krohn* PRODUCT PHOTOGRAPHER: *Assasi* CLIENT: *Nicola Restaurant* MANUFACTURER: *Abbott Enterprises* MATERIALS: *Steel Tubing, cotton/lycra fabric* DESIGN YEAR: *1993* PRODUCTION YEAR: *1993* LAUNCH YEAR: *1993*

PAGE 176 PRODUCT: *Floor Lamp* DESIGNER: *Harry Allen* MANUFACTURER: *Harry Allen & Associates* MATERIALS: *Metal, ceramic foam* DESIGN YEAR: *1994* PRODUCTION YEAR: *1994*

PAGE 177 (LEFT) PRODUCT: *Lucilla Suspension Light* DESIGNER: *Paulo Rizzatto* MANUFACTURER: *Luceplan S.p.A.* MATERIALS: *Nomex fabric, metal frame* DESIGN YEAR: *1992* PRODUCTION YEAR: *1996* LAUNCH YEAR: *1996*

PAGE 177 (RIGHT) PRODUCT: *Milk Bottle Lamp* DESIGN FIRM: *Droog Design* ART DIRECTOR: *Teake Bulstra* DESIGNER: *Tejo Remi* PRODUCT PHOTOGRAPHER: *Hans van der Mars* MANUFACTURER: *DMD* MATERIALS: *Stainless steel, glass milk bottles* DESIGN YEAR: *1993* PRODUCTION YEAR: *1995* LAUNCH YEAR: *1995*

PAGE 178 (TOP LEFT) DESIGNERS: *Peter Lynch, Dagmar Frinta* MATERIALS: *Cast Iron* DESIGN DATE: *3/97* PRODUCTION DATE: *4/97*

PAGE 178 (TOP RIGHT) PRODUCT: *Penumbra Floor Lamp* DESIGN FIRM/MANUFACTURER: *Office O* DESIGNER: *Todd Bracher* PRODUCT PHOTOGRAPHER: *Todd Bracher, Office O* DESIGN DATE: *4/96*

PAGE 179 PRODUCT: *Interlude Lamp* DESIGN FIRMS: *TZ Design, Jhane Barnes, DMJ Rottet* DESIGNERS: *Mark Goetz, Jhane Barnes, Mark Goetz* PRODUCT PHOTOGRAPHER: *Viewpoint Studios* MANUFACTURER: *Bernhardt* DESIGN DATE: *1/96* PRODUCTION DATE: *6/96* LAUNCH DATE: *6/96*

PAGE 180 (TOP) PRODUCT: *Levi's Silver Tab Suitcase* DESIGN FIRM: *Charles S. Anderson Design* ART DIRECTORS: *Charles Anderson* DESIGNERS: *Charles Anderson, Daniel Olson* ILLUSTRATORS: *Randall Dahlk CSA Archive* PRODUCT PHOTOGRAPHER: *Dave Bausman* CLIENT: *Levi Strauss*

PAGE 180 (BOTTOM) PRODUCT: *Suitcase* DESIGN FIRM: *FM Design Ltd.* ART DIRECTORS: *Richard Miles* DESIGNERS: *Ian Ferris, Roger Pedlar of FM Design;*

Rik Hillaert, Bob Tesman of Samsonite PRODUCT PHOTOGRAPHER: *Johnny Rutter* MANUFACTURER: *Samsonite Europe NV* MATERIALS: *Polypropylene* LAUNCH DATE: *3/95*

PAGE 181 (TOP, BOTTOM) PRODUCT: *Fujitsu Attaché Portable UNIX Workstation* DESIGN FIRM: *Machineart* MATERIAL: *Stitched leather*

PAGE 181 (MIDDLE) DESIGN FIRM: *Studio Oz* DESIGNER: *Lela Emmons* PRODUCT PHOTOGRAPHER: *John Bonath, Maddog Studio* MANUFACTURER: *Studio Oz* MATERIALS: *Aluminum, steel* DESIGN DATE: *1/97* PRODUCTION DATE: *2/97*

PAGE 182 PRODUCT: *Low-Cost Kneebrace* DESIGN FIRM: *designDESIGN* PRODUCT PHOTOGRAPHER: *Tom Page Photography* CLIENT: *Smith & Nephew/Donjoy* MATERIALS: *Aluminum, elastomer, ABS, nylon webbing* DESIGN YEAR: *1994* PRODUCTION YEAR: *1995* LAUNCH YEAR: *1995*

PAGE 183 (TOP) PRODUCT: *Toothbrush for Children* DESIGN FIRM: *Smart Design, Inc.* ART DIRECTOR: *Tom Dair* DESIGNERS: *Vanessa Sica, Mari Ando, Paul Hamburger* PRODUCT PHOTOGRAPHER: *Peter Medliek* CLIENT: *Johnson & Johnson* MANUFACTURER: *Johnson & Johnson* MATERIALS: *Polypropylene, elastomer* DESIGN DATE: *12/95* PRODUCTION DATE: *6/96* LAUNCH DATE: *6/96*

PAGE 183 (BOTTOM) PRODUCT: *PC 200 Plaque Removal Instrument* DESIGN FIRM: *Machineart* DESIGNER: *Andrew Serbinski* PRODUCT PHOTOGRAPHER: *Mark Jenkinson* MANUFACTURER: *Teledyne Water Pik* MATERIALS: *ABS* DESIGN YEAR: *1994* PRODUCTION YEAR: *1995* LAUNCH YEAR: *1995*

PAGE 184 PRODUCT: *Dinamap Select Patient Monitor* DESIGN FIRM: *Hauser, Inc.* ART DIRECTOR: *Ron Pierce* DESIGNERS: *Edward Cruz, Ernesto Quinteros, David Hoard, Andy Hooper* PRODUCT PHOTOGRAPHER: *Terry Sutherland, Sutherland Photo Design* CLIENT: *Johnson & Johnson Medical Inc.* MATERIALS: *Die-cast magnesium, injection-molded elastomer* PRODUCTION YEAR: *1996* LAUNCH YEAR: *6/96*

PAGE 185 PRODUCT: *Medical Chair* DESIGN FIRM: *Karo Design Resources, Inc.* DESIGNERS: *Greg Corrigan, Barry Marshall, Nick Nolo* PRODUCT PHOTOGRAPHER: *Tony Redpath* CLIENT: *Current Technology Corporation* MANUFACTURER: *Demed Mfg.* MATERIALS: *Fiberglass sheet metal, thermoformed parts* DESIGN DATE: *1/91* PRODUCTION DATE: *4/96* LAUNCH DATE: *4/96*

PAGE 186 PRODUCT: *Stacking Letter Tray* DESIGN FIRM: *ROGOV International Design* DESIGNER: *Vladymir Rogov* PRODUCT PHOTOGRAPHER: *Kevin Halle* MANUFACTURER: *Arkitex Productions, Inc.* MATERIALS: *ABS* DESIGN DATE: *5/95* PRODUCTION DATE: *1/97* LAUNCH DATE: *12/96*

PAGE 187 PRODUCT: *Grip Stand Up Stapler* CLIENT: *Boston* MATERIALS: *Plastic housing, all-steel mechanism*

PAGE 188 PRODUCT: *Letter Opener* DESIGN FIRM: *Ecco Design, Inc.* DESIGNERS: *Eric Chan, Yoon Ho Chio* PRODUCT PHOTOGRAPHER: *Ecco Design, Inc.* MANUFACTURER: *Hoyo Inc.* MATERIALS: *Stamped Steel* DESIGN YEAR: *1995* PRODUCTION YEAR: *1996* LAUNCH YEAR: *1996*

PAGE 189 PRODUCT: *X 2000 X-Acto Knife* DESIGN FIRM: *Ecco Design Inc.* DESIGNERS: *Eric Chan, Eyal Eliva, Jeff Miller* PRODUCT PHOTOGRAPHER: *Ecco Design Inc.* MANUFACTURER: *Hunt Manufacturing Corporation* MATERIALS: *Insert-molded santoprene* DESIGN YEAR: *1994* PRODUCTION YEAR: *1995* LAUNCH YEAR: *1996*

PAGES 190, 191 PRODUCT: *Copier and Stand* DESIGN FIRM: *Stuart Karten Design* DESIGNERS: *Stuart Karten, Paul Kirley, Michael Rocha, Dennis Schroeder* PRODUCT PHOTOGRAPHER: *Henry Blackham* MANUFACTURER: *Abex Display Systems* DESIGN DATE: *8/96* PRODUCTION DATE: *3/97* LAUNCH DATE: *4/97*

PAGE 192 PRODUCT: *Computer Accessories* DESIGN FIRM: *Bernstein Design Associates* DESIGNERS: *Harvey Bernstein of Bernstein Design Associates, Noel Zeller of Zelco Industries* PRODUCT PHOTOGRAPHER: *Marc Russell* MANUFACTURER: *Zelco Industries, Inc.* MATERIALS: *Polypropylene* DESIGN DATE: *1/96* PRODUCTION DATE: *3/96*

PAGE 193 PRODUCT: *PC Gear Ergo Comfort Mousepad and Mouse Cord Manager* DESIGN FIRM: *EXO Design* DESIGNER: *Ron Boeder* PRODUCT PHOTOGRAPHER:

Don Corning MANUFACTURER: *Pantech Internaitonal* MATERIALS: *Injection-molded ABS* DESIGN DATE: *5/96* PRODUCTION DATE: *5/96* LAUNCH DATE: *6/96*
PAGE 194, 195 PRODUCT: *Surfboard* DESIGN FIRM: *Simon & Goetz* ART DIRECTOR: *Rüdiger Goetz* CLIENT: *ON DIREKT* DESIGN DATE: *3/96*

PAGE 196 PRODUCT: *Prototype Portable Spectator Seat* DESIGNER: *Jennifer Gibbs* PRODUCT PHOTOGRAPHER: *Miho Suzuke* MATERIALS: *Tubular aluminum, nylon fabric, foam* DESIGN DATE: *3/96* PRODUCTION DATE: *3/96*

PAGE 197 (TOP) PRODUCT: *Lofox Bicycle Helmet* DESIGN FIRM: *Design Workshop* DESIGNERS: *John Tutton, Mike Sirois, Rod Muir, Jerome Foy* PRODUCT PHOTOGRAPHER: *Steven Fenn* MANUFACTURER: *Safe Cycle* MATERIALS: *EPP liners, Carome 49 shell, polyethylene foam comfort liner, polypropelene webbing* DESIGN YEAR: *1994* PRODUCTION YEAR: *1995* LAUNCH YEAR: *1995*

PAGE 197 (BOTTOM) PRODUCT: *R 180 S Ski Goggles* DESIGN FIRM: *Designworks/USA* DESIGNERS: *Andy Vong, Jonathon Dry, Dave Robran* MANUFACTURER: *Scott USA*

PAGE 198 PRODUCT: *Binoculars* DESIGN FIRM: *Altitude* ART DIRECTOR: *Alan Ball* DESIGNER: *Thomas Swyst* PRODUCT PHOTOGRAPHER: *Thomas Swyst, Altitude* CLIENT: *VU Points* MANUFACTURER: *VU Points* MATERIALS: *Injection-molded PC/ABS blend for housing; injection-molded Kraton grip, eye cups, visors; printed Lexan In-Mold-Decoration film; sewn faux-suede/polypropylene webbing strap; VIA overmolded elastomeric grip* DESIGN YEAR: *1995* PRODUCTION YEAR: *1995* LAUNCH YEAR: *1995*

PAGE 199 PRODUCT: *Night Mariner* DESIGN FIRM: *Bolt* ART DIRECTOR: *Edgar Montague* DESIGNERS: *Mark Gildesleeve, Dennis Huguley* PRODUCT PHOTOGRAPHER: *Steve Knight* MANUFACTURER: *ITT* MATERIALS: *Santoprene TPR, ABS* DESIGN DATE: *6/92* PRODUCTION DATE: *2/93* LAUNCH DATE: *2/93*

PAGES 200, 201 PRODUCT: *Power Grip Shifter* DESIGN FIRM: *Designworks/USA* DESIGNERS: *Niko von Saurma, Marc Tappeiner, John Cook, Randy Lewis, Christian Battlogg, Marcus Arbaiter, Peter Deuling, Jonathan Wiant* PRODUCT PHOTOGRAPHER: *Darren Yasukochi* MANUFACTURER: *Fichtel & Sachs AG* DESIGN DATE: *6/95* PRODUCTION DATE: *4/96* LAUNCH DATE: *7/96*

PAGE 201 PRODUCT: *Ergo Tech Grip and System 3 Baskets* DESIGN FIRM: *DesignWorks/USA* CLIENT: *Scott* MATERIAL: *Shock-absorbing elastomer*

PAGE 202 (TOP) PRODUCT: *Swim Fins* DESIGN FIRM/MANUFACTURER: *Bob Evans Designs Inc.* DESIGNER: *Bob Evans* PRODUCT PHOTOGRAPHER: *Bob Evans* MATERIALS: *Polyurethane*

PAGE 202 (BOTTOM) PRODUCT: *Sports Shoe* DESIGN FIRM: *Sports Creative, Inc.* DESIGNERS: *Tom Foxen, Charles Johnson* PRODUCT PHOTOGRAPHER: *John Moldauer, Phototown* CLIENT: *Benetton Sportsystem* MATERIALS: *Leather, polyurethane, rubber, steel* DESIGN DATE: *5/95* LAUNCH DATE: *11/96*

PAGE 203 PRODUCT: *Sports Shoe* DESIGN FIRM: *Sports Creative, Inc.* DESIGNER: *Charles Johnson* PRODUCT PHOTOGRAPHER: *Michael Watson* CLIENT: *Prince Sports Group* MATERIALS: *Leather, Pebax, polyurethane, rubber* DESIGN DATE: *12/94* PRODUCTION DATE: *5/95* LAUNCH DATE: *10/95*

PAGE 204 PRODUCT: *Bicycle Wheel* DESIGN FIRM: *Spinergy* DESIGNER: *Raphael Schlanger* PRODUCT PHOTOGRAPHER: *Greg Wostrel* MANUFACTURER: *Spinergy* DESIGN YEAR: *1992* PRODUCTION YEAR: *1994* LAUNCH YEAR: *1994*

PAGE 205 (TOP) PRODUCT: *Rotwild Mountain Bike* DESIGN FIRM: *Simon & Goetz* DESIGNER: *Rüdiger Goetz* MANUFACTURER: *adp.engineering GmbH*

PAGE 205 (BOTTOM) PRODUCT: *Mountain Bike* DESIGN FIRM: *Art Center College of Design, Pasadena* DESIGNERS: *Fridolin Beisert, Michael Sans* PRODUCT PHOTOGRAPHER: *Steven Heller*

PAGE 206 PRODUCT: *Kayak* DESIGN FIRM: *Kayak Lab, Inc.* DESIGNER: *Vit Pesikov* PRODUCT PHOTOGRAPHER: *Vit Pesikov* MANUFACTURER: *Kayak Lab* MATERIALS: *Tubular aluminum*

space frame DESIGN YEAR: *1994* PRODUCTION YEAR: *1995* LAUNCH DATE: *1/96*
PAGE 207 PRODUCT: *Wrist Watches* DESIGN FIRM: *Graves Design* ART DIRECTOR: *Michael Graves* CLIENT: *Projects*

PAGE 208 (TOP) PRODUCT: *Wrist Watches* DESIGN FIRM: *Graves Design* DESIGNER: *Michael Graves* PRODUCT PHOTOGRAPHER: *Marek Bulaj, Michael Graves Architect* CLIENT: *The Markuse Corporation* MANUFACTURER: *D'objects Moderenes* MATERIALS: *Aluminum with leather band* DESIGN DATE: *2/96* PRODUCTION DATE: *8/96* LAUNCH DATE: *9/96*

PAGE 208 (BOTTOM) PRODUCT: *Touching Watch (for the blind)* DESIGN FIRM: *BOD Design* DESIGNERS: *Shin-Chun "David" Wang, Dr. Shyh-Jye Wang* PRODUCT PHOTOGRAPHER: *Shin-Chun "David" Wang* MATERIALS: *Silicon rubber, stainless steel, POS* DESIGN YEAR: *1995* DESIGN YEAR: *1996*

PAGE 209 (TOP) PRODUCT: *Clock* DESIGN FIRM: *Sigmag* DESIGNER: *Luke Raymond* PRODUCT PHOTOGRAPHER: *Cynthia Greig* MANUFACTURER: *Luke Raymond* MATERIALS: *Aluminum* DESIGN DATE: *1/97* PRODUCTION DATE: *1/97* LAUNCH DATE: *1/97*

PAGE 209 (BOTTOM) PRODUCT: *Employee Gift Clock* DESIGN FIRM: *CKS Partners* ARTISTIC DIRECTOR: *Siras Greiner* DESIGNER: *Alex Willard* PRODUCT PHOTOGRAPHER: *Daniel DeSouza* CLIENT: *Pixar Animation Studios*

PAGE 210 PRODUCT: *A Homogenous Clock* DESIGN FIRM: *Dunay & Albright Architects* DESIGNERS: *Donna Dunay, Robert Dunay* PRODUCT PHOTOGRAPHER: *Robert Dunay* MANUFACTURER: *Emory Shaver* MATERIALS: *Aluminum* PRODUCTION DATE: *2/95*

PAGE 211 (TOP LEFT, TOP RIGHT) PRODUCT: *Joe Boxer Wrist Watch* DESIGN FIRM: *Smart Design* DESIGNERS: *Debbie Hahn, Paul Hamburger, Stephanie Kim, Tucker Viemeister* PRODUCT PHOTOGRAPHER: *Peter Medilek, Claus Associates* MANUFACTURER: *Waterbury Watch Company*

PAGE 211 (BOTTOM LEFT) PRODUCT: *Watchdog Watch* DESIGN FIRM: *C.S. Anderson Design* DESIGNER: *Todd Piper-Hauswirth* PRODUCT PHOTOGRAPHER: *Paul Irmitar* CLIENT: *Paramount/Fujisankei* FACE PRINTER: *KEA, Inc.*

PAGE 212 PRODUCT: *Virtual Image Clock* DESIGN FIRM/MANUFACTURER: *Electrokinetics, Inc.* DESIGNERS: *Leo Fernekes, Stefan Rublowsky* PRODUCT PHOTOGRAPHER: *Catherine McGlynn* MATERIALS: *Aluminum, steel, plastic, electronics* DESIGN DATE: *8/93* PRODUCTION DATE: *2/1/97* LAUNCH DATE: *5/17/97*

PAGE 213 PRODUCT: *Moment Series Wrist Watches* DESIGN FIRM: *Alan Chan Design Company* DESIGNERS: *Alan Chan, Peter Lo, Phillip Leung* CLIENT: *Alan Chan Creations Ltd.*

PAGE 214, 215 PRODUCT: *Kawasaki Mk9* DESIGN FIRM: *Machineart* DESIGNER: *Andrew Serbinski* PRODUCT PHOTOGRAPHER: *Mark Jenkinson* MANUFACTURER: *Machineart* MATERIALS: *Fiberglass, aluminum, stainless steel* DESIGN YEAR: *1994* PRODUCTION YEAR: *1995* LAUNCH DATE: *2/96*

PAGE 216 PRODUCT: *Motorcycle* DESIGN FIRM: *Studio Martone* ART DIRECTOR: *Jim Martin* PRODUCT PHOTOGRAPHER: *Jim Martin*

PAGE 216 PRODUCT: *BMW R 1100 RT* DESIGN FIRM/MANUFACTURER: *BMW AG*

PAGE 217 PRODUCT: *BMW Z3* DESIGN FIRM/MANUFACTURER: *BMW AG*

PAGE 218 PRODUCT: *Mercedes-Benz SL Sport* DESIGN FIRM: *Mercedes-Benz*

PAGE 219 PRODUCT: *VW Beetle* DESIGN FIRM: *SHR Perceptual Management* DESIGNER: *J. Mays* PRODUCT PHOTOGRAPHER: *Rodney Rascona* MANUFACTURER: *Volkswagen AG* DESIGN YEAR: *1993* LAUNCH YEAR: *1997-1998*

PAGE 220 DESIGN FIRM: *Art Center College of Design, Pasadena* DESIGNER: *Ryan Church* PRODUCT PHOTOGRAPHER: *Steven Heller, Art Center College of Design, Pasadena*

INDEX

VERZEICHNIS

INDEX

. . . .
P H O T O G R A P H E R S
. . . .

G R A P H I S   B O O K S

Graphis 305   Johnson Conran IKEA Mead Show Grundy & Northedge Slover Tachibana

Graphis 305

Graphis 304   Schwab Illustrators Demarchelier Koolhaas Kosolapov Stolichnaya Troxler

Graphis 304

Graphis 303   Makela Lewis Moberly Sagmeister Nowland Fallon McElligott Berlin Haase & Kneis

Graphis 303

G R A P H I S   M A G A Z I N E

MAGAZINE	USA	CANADA	SOUTHAMERICA/ ASIA/PACIFIC
☐ ONE YEAR (6 ISSUES)	US$ 89.00	US$ 99.00	US$ 125.00
☐ TWO YEARS (12 ISSUES)	US$ 159.00	US$ 179.00	US$ 235.00
☐ AIRMAIL SURCHARGE (6 ISSUES)	US$ 59.00	US$ 59.00	US$ 59.00

☐ CHECK ENCLOSED (PAYABLE TO GRAPHIS)   ☐ BILL ME

USE CREDIT CARDS TO PAY IN US DOLLARS

☐ AMERICAN EXPRESS   ☐ MASTERCARD   ☐ VISA

CARD NO.   EXP. DATE

CARDHOLDER NAME

SIGNATURE

(PLEASE PRINT)

NAME

TITLE

COMPANY

ADDRESS

CITY

STATE/PROVINCE   ZIP CODE

COUNTRY

SEND ORDER FORM AND MAKE CHECK PAYABLE TO:
GRAPHIS INC., 141 LEXINGTON AVENUE, NEW YORK, NY 10016-8193

SERVICE BEGINS WITH ISSUE THAT IS CURRENT WHEN ORDER IS PROCESSED.

MAGAZINE	EUROPE/AFRICA MIDDLE EAST	GERMANY	U.K.
☐ ONE YEAR (6 ISSUES)	SFR. 164.–	DM 190,–	£ 68.00
☐ TWO YEARS (12 ISSUES)	SFR. 295.–	DM 342,–	£ 122.00

SUBSCRIPTION FEES INCLUDE POSTAGE AND PACKAGING

☐ AIRMAIL SURCHARGE (6 ISSUES)	SFR. 65.–	DM 75,–	£ 30.00
☐ REGISTERED MAIL (6 ISSUES)	SFR. 20.–	DM 24,–	£ 9.00

FOR CREDIT CARD PAYMENT (ALL CARDS DEBITED IN SWISS FRANCS):

☐ AMERICAN EXPRESS   ☐ DINER'S CLUB

☐ EURO/MASTERCARD   ☐ VISA/BARCLAYCARD/CARTE BLEUE

CARD NO.   EXP. DATE

CARDHOLDER NAME

SIGNATURE

☐ CHECK ENCLOSED (MAKE SFR.-CHECK PAYABLE TO A SWISS BANK)
☐ BILL ME
☐ STUDENTS MAY REQUEST A 25% DISCOUNT BY SENDING STUDENT ID

(PLEASE PRINT)

LAST NAME   FIRST NAME

TITLE

COMPANY

ADDRESS

CITY   POSTAL CODE

COUNTRY

NOTE TO GERMAN SUBSCRIBERS ONLY:
ICH ERKLÄRE MICH EINVERSTANDEN, DASS MEINE NEUE ADRESSE
DURCH DIE POST AN DEN VERTRIEB WEITERGELEITET WIRD.
SEND ORDER FORM AND MAKE CHECK PAYABLE TO: DESIGN BOOKS
INTERNATIONAL, DUFOURSTRASSE 107, CH-8008 ZÜRICH, SWITZERLAND

SERVICE BEGINS WITH ISSUE THAT IS CURRENT WHEN ORDER IS PROCESSED.

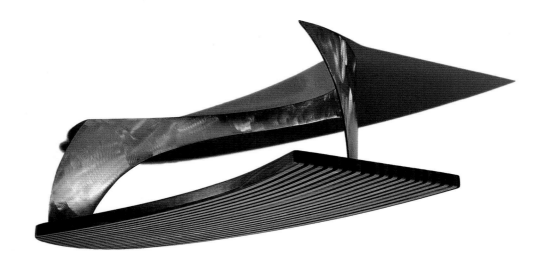